THE
XI JINPING
THOUGHT
NOW

HS PRESS

THE XI JINPING THOUGHT NOW

RYUHO OKAWA

HS PRESS

Contents

The Xi Jinping Thought Now

7   **The Cosmic Battle between Light and Darkness behind Earth's History**

8 What Is the "Xi Jinping Thought" Regarding China?

11　After Recording "the Xi Jinping Thought Now"

Afterword

In this book, there are a total of four interviewers from Happy Science, symbolized as A, B, C, and D, in the order that they first appear.

Preface

It would be nice to get along well with our neighbors. But there are times when we have dangerous neighbors, making our lives very difficult.

This book investigates whether the nature of Mr. Xi Jinping's way of thinking has changed after Mr. Biden from the Democratic Party won the U.S. presidential election. Those who have read my books in the past may find it easy to understand, whereas those who read my book for the first time may feel puzzled or bewildered by it.

People in power tend to expand their desires to control others. However, when we consider the future of the Earth civilization, there must be limits to how much a country is allowed to do to govern its people and how much it is allowed to meddle in other countries' affairs.

Now, I am thinking about how Earth should be in this vast universe. I believe the time has come to unveil the "dark being" behind the Xi Jinping Thought.

Ryuho Okawa
Master & CEO of Happy Science Group
March 2, 2021

The Xi Jinping Thought Now

*Originally recorded in Japanese on February 5, 2021
at the Special Lecture Hall of Happy Science in Japan
and later translated into English*

Xi Jinping (1953 - Present)

Xi Jinping is a politician of the People's Republic of China. He is a member of the "Crown Prince Party"—a group of descendants of prominent Chinese Communist party leaders. In 2008, the National People's Congress elected him vice president of China. In 2012, Xi Jinping became chairman of the CPC Central Military Commission, which named him the successor of President Hu Jintao. In 2013, he was elected President of the People's Republic of China.

1

How the Title of
This Spiritual Interview Was Decided

RYUHO OKAWA

Today, I would like to summon the guardian spirit of President Xi Jinping of China. So far, Happy Science has published seven books of spiritual interviews with him, so he is very "popular," or should I say, people want to know about his thoughts.

It may be partly because of the results of the U.S. presidential election, but I cannot help sensing that he is becoming very powerful now. I don't know whether it is the last world emperor or the eternal world emperor, but he probably believes himself to be something like that.

Today's title was specified by him (Xi's guardian spirit). He said he would accept the interview if it was titled, "The Xi Jinping Thought Now." In fact, we were planning to hold a spiritual interview with him yesterday, but because I had titled it "Boastful Laughter of Xi Jinping," he apparently felt insulted or profaned, making it difficult for us to proceed with the interview. For the rest of the day, I felt strange entities coming to bother me.

So today, we'd like to adopt a slightly humbler attitude and openheartedly listen to the opinions of the "great one." I hope you will listen carefully to what he has to say. Perhaps his opinions should only be revealed to the people of China, but this interview will also provide extremely important guidelines to the people of Japan, a neighboring country, especially when considering future Japan-China relations.

We, Happy Science, have no intention of using Mr. Xi Jinping (his guardian spirit) for our own purposes. Instead, we hope to fulfill the role of "nicely" conveying the current thoughts of a person who could be called the "world emperor" to the people of Japan, Taiwan, Hong Kong, Europe, the U.S., and also mainland China. I would appreciate it if he could tell us his honest opinions.

[*Claps once.*] Now, the guardian spirit of President Xi Jinping of China, the guardian spirit of President Xi Jinping of China, please come down to Happy Science and tell us what kind of thoughts Xi Jinping has in his mind now. We would appreciate it if you could tell us the Xi Jinping Thought now, or what he is thinking.

[*About 25 seconds of silence.*]

2

How China Overcame the Coronavirus

"China's 1.4 billion people will become leaders to create the future of the world"

XI JINPING'S GUARDIAN SPIRIT

Hmm... Hmm... Hmm! [*Clicks tongue.*] Hmm! What an annoying group.

A

Good morning. Are you President Xi Jinping?

XI JINPING'S G.S.

You are such a nuisance, just like flies buzzing around.

A

We're sorry.

XI JINPING'S G.S.

Hmm.

A

The year 2021 is the 100th anniversary of the founding of the Chinese Communist Party (CCP). We are honored to be able to interview President Xi Jinping before the upcoming Chinese New Year.

XI JINPING'S G.S.
OK.

A

From the beginning of this year, we have been experiencing a time of upheaval across the entire Earth. We would be grateful if President Xi Jinping could give us, humankind, some kind of...

XI JINPING'S G.S.
Humankind?

A

Yes... some guidelines for this year.

XI JINPING'S G.S.
Humankind has entered an era in which the 1.4 billion

Chinese people will become leaders and unite to create the future of the world. This is the meaning of the 100th anniversary of the CCP.

The reason China has suffered less from the coronavirus

A

Last year, the coronavirus widely spread across the world. However, you stated in your 2021 New Year address that China overcame the impact of the pandemic and made great achievements both in coordinating disease prevention and control and in economic and social development. So, the first thing other countries are eager to know is how China conquered the pandemic. We would appreciate it if you would share your wisdom on this matter.

XI JINPING'S G.S.

China is the most advanced nation in the world now. I don't know how things are in the "underdeveloped" countries. I know there is one such country in which 26 million people were infected (at the time of the recording). But China suffered only a small amount of damage because we run our nation based on scientific thinking. It's this scientific thinking that made the difference.

The (former) U.S. president insisted on not wearing a mask, despite the fact that many people were dying in his country. It was as if he was leading by example and rushing toward death.

On the other hand, we shut down Wuhan, a city with a population of 11 million people, immediately after the coronavirus was found and destroyed the virus all at once. While there is still some backflow of the virus coming from overseas, China has basically overcome the pandemic and is now moving toward further development.

A

As a prerequisite to overcoming the coronavirus, I think the cause of the virus needs to be identified. What was the cause of the coronavirus, after all?

XI JINPING'S G.S.

Viruses have existed in every age. Infectious diseases have spread in every era. It's important to figure out how to integrate the concept of hygiene and scientific thinking.

We also need mobility—the nation's mobility and the power to take decisive action. Those are important.

"To overcome the coronavirus, you should arrest all people enjoying nightlife"

A

How can other nations, for example Japan, overcome the pandemic?

XI JINPING'S G.S.

The infection rate isn't that high in Japan.

The number of infected people is about four times that of China, or over 40 times that of China based on the population ratio (at the time of the recording). This is because Japanese people go out to enjoy nightlife too much.

You just need to make a mass arrest if people go out at night. Why are the foolish politicians wasting time by discussing bills in the Diet? They just need to arrest everyone walking around on the streets after 8 p.m.

A

Just arrest them?

XI JINPING'S G.S.

Yes, then it will be over.

A

That's a very simple idea.

XI JINPING'S G.S.

Yes, it is. If the prisons become too full, you can just sink them into Tokyo Bay.

A

Is that how you actually deal with matters in China?

XI JINPING'S G.S.

Of course. If you can't bury them all in the ground, you need to find somewhere else to bury them.

A

In the early stages of the outbreak, the number of infected people increased dramatically in China as well. So, do you mean that you removed all those people at that time?

XI JINPING'S G.S.

My "strong admonishment" scared all the coronavirus away. That's just how it happened.

A

I see.

Lying about Americans spreading the malignant virus near the lab

A

The Chinese government has been controlling information quite tightly. Do you have anything to say about that?

XI JINPING'S G.S.

We control information because it's common for misinformation to delude people. There is a possibility of foreign spies spreading false information to create confusion within a nation. Some insurgents may see this as an opportunity to revolt, so I made sure to remove all such potential dangers. Because the citizens focused on fighting to eliminate the coronavirus together, we were able to end the problem in a couple of months.

A
Why was it that the coronavirus infection increased so explosively in Wuhan in the beginning?

XI JINPING'S G.S.
Huh? Well, at the time, American people were still able to travel to China. Because we have a laboratory there, they probably dispersed the malignant virus nearby.

A
Are you saying it was the Americans who spread the virus?

XI JINPING'S G.S.
Yes. They did it to set China up as the culprit. In that sense, we are too "nice."

3

Manipulating the U.S. Presidential Election

Electing Mr. Biden "was the absolutely correct judgment for a mobocracy"

A

Let me change the topic of conversation. There was a presidential election in the U.S. late last year. How did you predict the election to develop? And what do you think about the outcome of the election?

XI JINPING'S G.S.

Well, I think it was meant to be that way. American people made the right decision. Although it may not be called a democracy, they made the right decision as a "mobocracy" and chose Biden and eliminated Trump. I think it was the absolutely correct judgment for a mobocracy.

A

I see. But you didn't immediately send your congratulations to Mr. Biden, did you?

XI JINPING'S G.S.

Hmm? Didn't I?

A

There was some speculation, or news reports, on why the Chinese government was not congratulating Mr. Biden at the time. Did you have any intention of not doing so?

XI JINPING'S G.S.

That's because they (the U.S.) were still arguing.

A

Does that mean you thought Trump could overturn the election results?

XI JINPING'S G.S.

No way. It was nothing like that [*laughs*].

"I didn't expect things to work out as perfectly as we had wanted"

B

Would you tell us the reason why you were so confident that Mr. Trump had no chance of winning?

XI JINPING'S G.S.

I never thought Trump didn't have a chance. I was of course thinking of what I would do in case Trump won the election. However, I honestly didn't expect things to work out as perfectly as we had wanted.

B

Do you mean you succeeded in playing the moves you had in mind?

XI JINPING'S G.S.

Yes, I guess we did.

B

Would you tell us a little more specifically about the moves you made?

XI JINPING'S G.S.

Well, you Japanese people may be able to read some Chinese classics, but not a single American is educated enough to read Chinese classics because they themselves have no history whatsoever. They are just stupid. Their only good trait is that they were stronger than the Native Americans.

China, on the other hand, is a treasure trove of tactics and strategies. Everyone is a strategist, so we are not an opponent the U.S. can compete with in the first place.

B

Various strategies, which you just spoke of, can be found in *The Art of War* by Sun Tzu.

XI JINPING'S G.S.

Yes, yes.

B

It covers an extensive collection of strategies, including financial assistance and infiltration of spies. In your case, what kinds of strategies and tactics did you use?

XI JINPING'S G.S.

The Art of War by Sun Tzu is available to the public and might have been translated into English. But in China, there are many other strategies that have not been translated.

B

We would really appreciate it if you could disclose some of the strategies that have not been translated.

XI JINPING'S G.S.

What? Well, pretending to lose ground against the U.S. when in fact I have already been the world emperor for 10 years is one of my strategies.

"I mobilized our whole nation to push the Biden side and sink the Trump side"

C

Do you mean you have the power to manipulate the U.S. presidential election?

XI JINPING'S G.S.

It was surprisingly easy.

B

Easy?

XI JINPING'S G.S.

I didn't expect it to be so simple. It must have been easy because it was a simple choice between the two people.

B

Of the strategies you tried, which did you find to be most effective?

XI JINPING'S G.S.

That's simple. We just pushed the side supporting Biden, while we sunk the side criticizing Biden. We advertised that the people supporting Trump were insane, whereas the people criticizing Trump held the correct opinion. We mobilized our whole nation based on this strategy.

B

You mentioned four points just now. First, how did you actually push the side that supported Biden?

XI JINPING'S G.S.

An American president who does nothing is the best president. That's it. So, we praised him as if he were the representative of good people in the world.

B

Does that mean you see Mr. Biden as the president who does nothing?

XI JINPING'S G.S.

Well, he does breathe.

B

So you think he just breathes?

XI JINPING'S G.S.

He does, and that's enough.

B

That's enough?

XI JINPING'S G.S.

Yes. He exhales carbon dioxide a little, but that can't be helped. Trump is no good because he comes up with unnecessary ideas.

"We eliminated Trump's allies one by one and even went after Hollywood"

B

What do you mean by "unnecessary ideas"? Can you give us some examples?

XI JINPING'S G.S.

He tried using cunning American strategies that were used a few hundred years ago, such as fighting a guerilla war against the U.K. or fighting the Native Americans. But he can't defeat China anyway.

B

President Xi does not fight in the same way a guerrilla war was fought a few hundred years ago, but tries to systematically dominate the entire world from every direction. Is that what you are saying?

XI JINPING'S G.S.

It's too obvious that the U.S. has been trying to contain China. However, Trump wasn't aware of the efforts that were being made to contain him. That's why he is a fool.

B

Can you tell us some of your containment efforts? How did you...

XI JINPING'S G.S.

We simply eliminated Trump's allies one by one. In the end, no one supported Trump. We made sure all the people who supported Trump would look like fanatics or blind followers.

B

Among the conservative people, there were many who seemed to be Trump's potential allies but ultimately changed their position. Did you do something to them, too?

XI JINPING'S G.S.

Yes.

Movie companies in Hollywood are trying to figure out how to create movies jointly with China. There are 900 million movie viewers in China, so movie companies could easily recoup their investments of hundreds of millions of dollars if they manage to attract the 900 million viewers. That's why they want to produce movies jointly with China and are trying hard to welcome more Chinese actors and actors of Chinese origin into Hollywood.

That's why Hollywood actors are supporting the Democratic Party and are trying their best to get along well with China. They are messengers of peace, indeed.

Trump has almost no allies, you know?

"We attacked Trump's biggest weakness, and it worked perfectly"

B

How did you see the Black Lives Matter movement, for example? Were you involved in that movement?

XI JINPING'S G.S.

Huh? It's hard to understand when you use English.

B

Their slogan means "Black people's lives are important."

XI JINPING'S G.S.

That's an obvious statement. Black people are important, and so are Asian people. Immigrants, women, and children are also important. That movement worked well.

B

What was impressive was how the focal theme of discussion shifted from black people to Asian people without people realizing it.

XI JINPING'S G.S.

That's a theme that Japanese people will also appreciate because they, too, have been victims. They have experienced discrimination based on their nationality. Japanese Americans were put in internment camps during World War II, and they must have suffered a lot in those times. Despite being American citizens, Japanese Americans were treated badly just because they were of Japanese origin. So, all we had to do was to remind them of that nightmare.

B

I see. So, in regard to how the theme of the movement spread to people of other races...

XI JINPING'S G.S.

Well, looking at it from a strategic standpoint, that was Trump's greatest weakness. Everyone felt that he was a racist, so it was important to expose that part of him.

B

So, you are saying you attacked that point?

XI JINPING'S G.S.

Yes. And it worked perfectly. All American mass media invested their energy into it.

"During Obama's presidency, China had already started a war against the U.S."

A

Based on what you have said, is it correct to assume that the war against the U.S. had already begun?

XI JINPING'S G.S.

We have been in war for more than 10 years already.

A

I see. So, you had started a war while the citizens of the U.S. had no idea that a war was happening.

XI JINPING'S G.S.

We were actually at war even during Obama's presidency. I doubt Obama thought of it in that way though.

B

Then, from China's perspective, you have already been in a state of war from 10 years ago.

XI JINPING'S G.S.

We worked very hard and made sure Obama received the Nobel Peace Prize.

B

Were you involved in that, too?

XI JINPING'S G.S.
Yes.

B
Then, did you approach the Nobel Committee as well?

XI JINPING'S G.S.
He received the Nobel Peace Prize soon after he took office, didn't he?

B
Right.

XI JINPING'S G.S.
He spoke of a world without nuclear weapons. That's a good thing, isn't it? If the U.S. continues to be a leading advocate of this idea, and if both the U.S. and Russia reduce their nuclear weapons, then there is no greater news for China.

B
Does this mean you made arrangements ahead of time, and Obama completely fell for the trap?

XI JINPING'S G.S.

Yes. We made sure Obama would get the Nobel Peace Prize and Trump wouldn't get one. Don't underestimate China's power.

China's plan to completely defeat the U.S. and gain hegemony

A

In that case, you must have decided on a final deadline for China's victory.

XI JINPING'S G.S.

Deadline? What do you mean by deadline?

A

Well, by when do you aim to gain hegemony over the world, or completely defeat the U.S.? For example, by 2050?

XI JINPING'S G.S.

We have to attain that while I'm in power.

A

While you are in power?

XI JINPING'S G.S.

Yes. China's presidential term used to be two five-year terms at most, but because I thought it would be difficult to accomplish my goals in 10 years, I abolished the limit. Now, I can remain the president indefinitely.

4

On the Strategies against Russia, the U.S., and Europe

China is "accelerating the anti-Putin movement"

B

Now, I'd like to ask you about topics of interest beyond this year.

XI JINPING'S G.S.

Yes, OK.

B

This will probably be a matter of discussion slightly after your initial 10-year term—maybe around 2025 or 2028—but the first point that the world is focusing on is Taiwan. What are your thoughts on Taiwan?

XI JINPING'S G.S.

They are too small and can be dealt with in any way. We could squash them like flies.

We are aiming for the downfall of the U.S. Although Russia is very difficult to handle, we are also accelerating the anti-Putin movement now. Putin may start getting in our way, especially because he has been in power for so long. We are currently thinking about removing Putin.

A

Is that also China's doing?

XI JINPING'S G.S.

Actually, there are times when we work with them. We sometimes cooperate with them regarding anti-American matters. But after the U.S. falls, Russia will be a little... hmm. Since they have a lot of nuclear weapons, it would be dangerous to let a long-serving dictator remain in power. We have to watch out for the danger behind us.

"America is over. Ousting Putin is our next goal"

B

Are you behind the movement currently occurring in Russia as well?

XI JINPING'S G.S.
Yes, we are.

B
Oh, you are?

XI JINPING'S G.S.
Of course.

B
In that case, Putin was originally in the KGB, so...

XI JINPING'S G.S.
Yes, I know.

B
He would surely anticipate your plan. What are your thoughts on that?

XI JINPING'S G.S.
What are you trying to say? All of China is the "KGB." So, we aren't afraid of anything [*laughs*]. Our entire nation is the "KGB"—not just the police but even the citizens are the "KGB" in China.

B

So, you are taking action while anticipating Putin to read your strategy, then?

XI JINPING'S G.S.

Even if he can read our strategy, he won't be able to do anything. It's impossible. We defeated Trump, so I believe we can do the same with Putin.

B

So, you think you can defeat Putin as well?

XI JINPING'S G.S.

Hmm, well, ousting Putin is our next goal.

A

In fighting the U.S., isn't it advantageous for China to ally with Russia?

XI JINPING'S G.S.

China and Russia? No, no. That's if the U.S. is strong.

A

So, you think the U.S. has already weakened and...

XI JINPING'S G.S.
After defeating Trump, next...

A
You have already won?

XI JINPING'S G.S.
Next, we have to defeat Russia. That's obvious if I am to be the world emperor.

A
I see. So, you are saying the U.S. is done.

XI JINPING'S G.S.
They are done.

A
Are they?

XI JINPING'S G.S.
Done. Yes, they are finished.

A
Finished?

XI JINPING'S G.S.

Yes. They are already finished.

Campaigning for Biden
to win the Nobel Peace Prize

A

But your country has been under economic sanctions...

XI JINPING'S G.S.

The U.S. will become a country like Mexico.

A

But the U.S. still has stronger military power than China.

XI JINPING'S G.S.

In regard to that, he will clean all of that up (by reducing their military power). We'll campaign again so that he can get a Nobel Peace Prize.

A

You mean Mr. Biden?

XI JINPING'S G.S.
Yes. We'll let the U.S. win another Nobel Peace Prize.

A
Ah...

XI JINPING'S G.S.
So, he just needs to get rid of all the nuclear weapons. Then, he'll get the Nobel Peace Prize. Yes.

"We will make the U.S. pay tribute to China"

A
But what about the economy?

XI JINPING'S G.S.
What do you mean?

A
In the New Year address (in 2021), you said that China also defeated severe floods, but there must have been some economic blow...

XI JINPING'S G.S.

If the U.S. becomes a country that receives guidance from China, the "advanced country," then they still have a chance to survive. Yes.

A

I see. So, in trading with the U.S., ...

XI JINPING'S G.S.

Ah, they should pay tribute to China.

A

You will make them pay tribute to China?

XI JINPING'S G.S.

Yes. That's right.

A

So, in terms of the economy...

XI JINPING'S G.S.

The U.S. should come to Beijing and ask us for instructions on what they should do every single time. So, from now on, they'll no longer be able to threaten us by saying things like they will increase the tariffs by 20 percent or 200 percent at their own discretion. It won't work.

A

It won't work that way.

XI JINPING'S G.S.

No.

"I intend to seize Europe and ultimately destroy the 'British Empire' completely"

A

So, you have already decided on how to deal with each country as a global strategy, then?

XI JINPING'S G.S.

Yes, that's right. Well, I intend to seize Europe, too...

A

Seize Europe?

XI JINPING'S G.S.

Ultimately, I intend to destroy the "British Empire" completely as well.

A

But Europe is also becoming anti-China because they suspect China is responsible for the coronavirus...

XI JINPING'S G.S.

That's fine. Europe will disappear while they are bickering.

A

How will they disappear?

XI JINPING'S G.S.

They will disappear. They will all die out, so it can't be helped.

B

Do you mean they will all die from the coronavirus?

XI JINPING'S G.S.

There are 100 million (infected) people now, aren't there?

China stopped at 100,000 people. We announced this number because I thought we needed to show that we suffered some damage. We've stopped at that level, but the world is at 100 million cases, right? Do you think it would take long for this number to reach one billion?

5

Talking about the Chinese State Secret of an Artificially Created Virus

"China has beings from the future as reinforcements"

B

It almost sounds like you anticipated, or rather knew ahead of time, that the coronavirus was going to spread, infect people, and mutate into new strains. According to some sources, the virus was deliberately engineered to mutate. Is this the way you saw things from the very beginning?

XI JINPING'S G.S.

I knew about all this.

B

So, you knew.

XI JINPING'S G.S.

Of course, I knew—we can foresee the future. We know how the future will unfold.

B

How are you able to know the future?

XI JINPING'S G.S.

Well, that's because we have reinforcements.

B

Ah. More specifically, what are these "reinforcements" that can see the future?

XI JINPING'S G.S.

There are beings that are designing the universe.

B

"There are beings that are designing the universe." Would you mind explaining this in a little more detail?

XI JINPING'S G.S.

Hmm... this is a confidential matter. It is a state secret, so...

B

I understand, but please...

XI JINPING'S G.S.

Well, we receive technology among other things.

B

Ah. Are you specifically being supplied with technology that allows you to see the future?

XI JINPING'S G.S.

There are beings from the future...

B

Oh, beings from the future.

XI JINPING'S G.S.

Yes, in China.

B

I see.

"Advanced technology was provided to China to create the virus"

A

This is news to us.

XI JINPING'S G.S.

Oh, is that so?

B

Yes. What is especially new to us is your awareness about beings from the future. In the previous spiritual interviews with Xi Jinping's guardian spirit, which are stacked up over there [*pointing at the books on Okawa's desk*], the guardian spirit back then didn't seem to understand much about either the space people from the future or the provisions of technology. You simply mentioned that it may be something your subordinates are dealing with. But do you, the guardian spirit speaking to us now, have a clear understanding of such matters?

XI JINPING'S G.S.

Well, Trump tried to disclose the space technology, so he had to be removed.

The technology we have is a different kind, but using it could greatly... Hmm... well, it's certainly a new "art of war." We have been receiving strategies that nobody knows about.

In regard to the recent virus, too, it required significantly advanced technology to design the virus so that it works differently depending on race.

B
So, you were provided with technology that enabled you to do so.

XI JINPING'S G.S.
Uh-huh.

A
Does that mean you know who the "being" is?

XI JINPING'S G.S.
Well... they helped us, so that's obvious.

A
They helped you?

XI JINPING'S G.S.
Uh-huh.

"Viruses were created for different countries"

A
Do you mean that the virus was first leaked in Wuhan?

XI JINPING'S G.S.
Well, what happened in Wuhan is a different story.

In fact, there's a different type for each race. It's very rare for a virus that works on Americans to work equally well on Indians. Indians are quite different from Americans.

B
So, you knew the being who provided the virus that would work on Indo-European genes?

XI JINPING'S G.S.
There are different kinds of viruses. We created them for different countries.

B

Ah, so you made different viruses for each country.

XI JINPING'S G.S.

More or less, yes. Well, I can't say we made viruses for all countries, but we made different kinds so each one would surely spread and be effective in the target country and the neighboring nations.

B

I see. A moment ago, you mentioned the U.K., which is reported to be somewhat at odds with China over matters such as the issue of Hong Kong.

XI JINPING'S G.S.

Right. We definitely need some (effective viruses) for the U.K. and the U.S.

B

So, you made the viruses not only to target the U.S. but also the U.K.?

XI JINPING'S G.S.

Yes. Comparing the landmass of the U.K. and its population, the amount of damage they are suffering is far too severe, no matter how you look at it.

B

Oh. So, the viral strain that started spreading last fall (2020), in particular, was part of such course of events?

XI JINPING'S G.S.

I made sure Japan got a smaller amount because Japan has the potential to be a useful "watchdog" for us in the future.

A

So, you are the one who made such a decision?

XI JINPING'S G.S.

Huh? Well, we think Japan is a potential watchdog. We can use Japan if they pay homage to us. Japan is still useful in dealing with the U.S., Europe, and other Asian, Islamic, and African countries. Yes.

6

About the Space Being Influencing Mr. Xi Jinping

Xi Jinping X, a being that aims to conquer Earth and become the "god of the universe"

B

This is a question I had prepared to ask you toward the end of this interview, but from what we've just heard, it feels like you are at a different "phase" compared to the guardian spirit that visited us previously. We understand that there is a space-related aspect incorporated into the thoughts and actions of Mr. Xi Jinping himself, and your awareness is somewhat...

XI JINPING'S G.S.

Er... try not to use English words so often, will you?

B

I mean, it seems you are at a different stage and your character has become somewhat advanced compared to before.

XI JINPING'S G.S.

Yes. I am simply showing a bit of my "claws," which I had been hiding.

A

Do you mean you've had these "claws" from the beginning?

XI JINPING'S G.S.

Yes. Well, someone as great as me... it's obvious, isn't it? I'm the one who is shining the most on Earth, so it's no surprise the beings in space would come to pay tribute to me.

B

Then, if there is a name to the spirit talking to us now, what should we call you?

XI JINPING'S G.S.

Huh?

B

Maybe you have a name you use in space.

XI JINPING'S G.S.

Hmm... Well, you can call me "Xi Jinping X." Yes.

A

Does the "X" mean you are keeping that part of the name a secret?

XI JINPING'S G.S.

Huh? Well, I am currently the world emperor, but apparently I am scheduled to become the "god of the universe" next. Hmm... yes... in the future.

A

You say "apparently," but who told you so?

XI JINPING'S G.S.

Hmm... Earth... well, I must first conquer Earth.

"My servants come from a planet located over two million light-years away"

A

Does that mean you have started to contact someone in space?

XI JINPING'S G.S.
Huh? I wouldn't call it "contact," but my many servants visit me.

A
Servants?

XI JINPING'S G.S.
Uh-huh.

A
For example?

XI JINPING'S G.S.
They travel a distance of two million light-years to visit me.

B
Ah, I see.

XI JINPING'S G.S.
Uh-huh.

A
What for?

XI JINPING'S G.S.
To help... To help us.

B
Two million light-years, and not 160,000 light-years... Wait. Isn't the place located two million light-years away Andromeda Galaxy?

XI JINPING'S G.S.
No, no. It's not necessarily Andromeda. Well, it tells me it comes from a planet with three suns.

B
Oh, I see.

XI JINPING'S G.S.
Uh-huh.

A
A planet with three suns. What is the planet called?

XI JINPING'S G.S.
Well, I can't disclose that to you.

A

You don't know? Is it a planet we haven't heard of?

XI JINPING'S G.S.

Xi Jinping X knows. Indeed.

A

Xi Jinping X knows.

XI JINPING'S G.S.

Yes. That's right.

Xi Jinping X had come during Genghis Khan's time as well

A

Are "Xi Jinping" and "Xi Jinping X" different? Are you the same?

XI JINPING'S G.S.

We are combined.

A&B
Combined?

XI JINPING'S G.S.
Yes, that's right.

A
What state is Xi Jinping's consciousness in right now?

XI JINPING'S G.S.
Of course, he has his own surface consciousness.

A
His own surface consciousness?

XI JINPING'S G.S.
Uh-huh.

A
Then, you mean his subconscious mind has already become Xi Jinping X?

XI JINPING'S G.S.
He, of course, also has a guardian spirit, but it's a little old.
So, it had to be replaced with a new one, didn't it?

A
Replace?

XI JINPING'S G.S.
Yes, the "software."

A
Does Xi Jinping's guardian spirit and Xi Jinping X share a
connection in terms of the soul?

XI JINPING'S G.S.
Yes, of course.

A
You do?

XI JINPING'S G.S.
Of course, we do. I was here when he founded the world
empire last time.

A

So, you were here during Genghis Khan's time?

XI JINPING'S G.S.

Hmm, the world... With Mongolia as the starting point, they placed the capital in China, conquered Europe, destroyed the Southern Song, and attacked as far as Japan. There is no way the Mongolians can do all that.

A

I see.

"After being attacked, we came to Earth in search of a home"

B

Then, you guided him at that time and have returned this time as well?

XI JINPING'S G.S.

I occasionally reappear.

B

Right. Then, where was your mother planet? Before you came here, where did you mainly live?

XI JINPING'S G.S.
Huh?

B

Where were you, specifically?

XI JINPING'S G.S.

I told you. The planet with three suns.

B

More specifically, what constellation or galaxy, for example, is "the planet with three suns" in? Will you tell us what you are referring to?

XI JINPING'S G.S.

Ah. Hmm... Well, you mentioned Andromeda Galaxy, but there is a different group from ours that resides in that galaxy. The group we are fighting on Earth is the same group we fought there, so we are now fighting a proxy war.

A

Do you know *Ame-no-Mioya-Gami*?

XI JINPING'S G.S.

Well, there might be someone who calls himself that. Hmm.

B

Based on what you said, it seems like you fought against space people on the side of *Ame-no-Mioya-Gami*, the God at the source of Japanese Shinto who came to Earth from Andromeda Galaxy 30,000 years ago, according to Happy Science's spiritual readings.

XI JINPING'S G.S.

So, our mother planet was severely attacked by those beings, and we came to Earth in search of another place to live. Hmm.

B

Ah. Do you mean you, Xi Jinping X, were originally also in Andromeda Galaxy but moved to another place?

XI JINPING'S G.S.

We have come to Earth because of a running battle. And they are also here.

B

You're saying the running battle has led them to Earth?

XI JINPING'S G.S.

They've come to Earth as well, and we are now fighting a proxy war here.

When did the switch from Xi Jinping to Xi Jinping X take place?

C

At what point did you switch from being Xi Jinping to Xi Jinping X, if there was ever such a point?

XI JINPING'S G.S.

Obviously, it was when I was ready to become the world emperor.

C

Speaking in terms of events on Earth, did your scenario develop significantly around the time of the U.S. presidential election?

XI JINPING'S G.S.

Trump was a somewhat formidable opponent. I thought I mustn't reveal my "real claws" until I defeated him. But I managed to bring him down.

In space proxy wars, Xi Jinping X fought against Greece, Egypt, and Japan

B

I'm afraid I have to go back to a previous point of discussion. You said you had moved away from Andromeda Galaxy, but because there was a running battle going on, the war is actually still continuing on Earth. Is this correct?

XI JINPING'S G.S.

Exactly.

B

In this running battle, how are you fighting the opponent?

XI JINPING'S G.S.

In the past, we created the Yuan dynasty and ruled Eurasia. We were defeated only once, when we attacked Japan during the Kamakura period (in the 13th century). That was the only time (we lost). I think the same enemies had reached out to Japan as well.

Before then, hmm... We fought a total war in efforts to destroy Greece.

Prior to that, we attacked Egypt in an attempt to destroy them. These instances are what remain in recorded history.

B

So, you fought them on those occasions.

XI JINPING'S G.S.

Yes, in those proxy wars.

B

You fought them in the form of a proxy war.

XI JINPING'S G.S.

We have been fighting a space proxy war.

Well, the war in Egypt was quite long. Egypt was fairly strong; it was an empire that lasted a long time.

A

Have you appeared and fought around Mesopotamia as well?

XI JINPING'S G.S.

Hmm... we were certainly there when it was at its greatest.

A

What do you mean by "at its greatest"?

XI JINPING'S G.S.

Well, we weren't exactly there, but we were guiding them.

A

You were guiding them?

XI JINPING'S G.S.

Hmm... Greece... So we were fighting to destroy democracy in Greece.

B

OK. So you guided Persia.

Is Ahriman, the god of darkness, one of the minions of Xi Jinping's guardian spirit?

A

Do you know Ahura Mazda, God of Light in Zoroastrianism?

XI JINPING'S G.S.

Oh, so you want to go that far back? That was even before we fought in Egypt.

A

Yes, it was before Egypt.

XI JINPING'S G.S.

Hmm.

A

How were you involved?

XI JINPING'S G.S.

Hmm... Hmm... I think we defeated them. Yes.

A

You defeated them?

XI JINPING'S G.S.

Yes. We defeated Zoroaster.

A

At that time, there was an opposing axis called Ahriman, who is said to be the god of darkness.

XI JINPING'S G.S.

Is that so? Ah. That Ahriman. Hmm.

A

Do you know Ahriman as well?

XI JINPING'S G.S.

Well... he is one of my minions.

A
A minion?

XI JINPING'S G.S.
Yes.

A
So, he's your minion.

XI JINPING'S G.S.
Yes. A minion. Well, I only recognized him as such.

B
Recently, we held a spiritual interview with Ahriman, and he said he is the boss [*laughs*]. (A spiritual interview with Ahriman was recorded on February 1, 2021.)

XI JINPING'S G.S.
Hahaha [*laughs*]. Whose boss? The question is whose boss he is.

B
He said Xi Jinping X or Xi Jinping is actually his minion.

XI JINPING'S G.S.

No way [*laughs*]. That's impossible. Right now, he is moving around Earth as "putrefying bacteria." So no, that's not possible. Although he might originally be from the universe, he has mostly been wandering aimlessly on Earth.

"We were defeated in Andromeda Galaxy and Planet Zeta, and we are now fighting on Earth"

B

It is said that Ahriman's group originated from the realm of hell on a planet in the Magellanic Clouds. Based on what we've heard from you, there seems to be a different group and…

XI JINPING'S G.S.

Well, we suffered a slight loss in Andromeda Galaxy. We then fought on Planet Zeta in the Magellanic Clouds—we had established a colony there, but a conflict occurred again. So we came to Earth, but they chased after us, which is why we are still in battle. Hmm.

Our two civilizations—I mean the civilization in Andromeda Galaxy and the civilization on Planet Zeta in the Magellanic Clouds—were destroyed by our adversaries, so we are currently fighting on Earth.

B

Does this mean your battle on Earth, in some ways, is the final battle?

XI JINPING'S G.S.

This isn't the only battle. We are fighting a few other battles elsewhere. We have separated into different groups.

A

This is not the only battle?

XI JINPING'S G.S.

No. What is happening on Earth is not the only battle, but only one of them. Just one of the battles.

A

So it's only one of them. More specifically, what are these other battles?

XI JINPING'S G.S.

Well, you know nothing about them, so there's no point in telling you.

7

The Cosmic Battle between Light and Darkness behind Earth's History

"The weak are destroyed
unless they pay tribute to us"

A

How would you describe this opposing axis, or your adversaries?

XI JINPING'S G.S.

Well [*clicks tongue*], they think differently than us. How should I put this? What we consider god is different from theirs.

A

How do they differ?

XI JINPING'S G.S.

Hmm. Their god teaches about feeble ideas such as love, mercy, and self-reflection, but it occasionally speaks of justice and exercises force. To us, their god is a strange, "androgynous" god. Our god is more masculine.

A
Could you explain a little about...

XI JINPING'S G.S.
The weak are destroyed.

A
The weak are destroyed?

XI JINPING'S G.S.
Yes. The strong prosper. Those who pay tribute are forgiven.

A
They are forgiven?

XI JINPING'S G.S.
Yes.

"The forces of darkness are the mainstream in the universe"

B

More specifically, what is the name of your (Xi Jinping X's) god?

XI JINPING'S G.S.

I am a god, too.

B

I'm sure you are, but since you mentioned, "our god," just a moment ago.

XI JINPING'S G.S.

Hmm. We consider ourselves to be in the mainstream in the universe, especially since it is mostly darkness out there. But there are forces trying to spread light in that environment. So, there is a need for a job to put out that light and make sure the universe does not get "burnt."

A

Is it fundamentally a logic of the dark side?

XI JINPING'S G.S.

What's wrong with that? The universe is pitch black, isn't it? We make up 80 percent of the universe.

A

Eighty percent?

XI JINPING'S G.S.

Yes.

"I want to get rid of the people who believe in Buddha, Christ, and Socrates"

A

I would also like to know if you are aware of the flip-side universe.

XI JINPING'S G.S.

This universe is the flip-side universe itself, isn't it?

A

The universe we are in now is the flip-side universe?

XI JINPING'S G.S.

Yes. It's dark, in principle. There is light only where there is a sun in the galaxy. Strange civilizations were born there, so we are now making sure their philosophies do not spread further. We are putting the fires out. We play the role of firefighters. The universe is meant to be dark and quiet.

B

However, in the history of Earth, I think you were only able to come to Earth when similar thought as yours collectively gathers on Earth to create a "hole," much like in current times or during the Yuan dynasty. Otherwise, you were unable to come. I heard it is normally quite difficult to intrude. What are your opinions on this?

XI JINPING'S G.S.

Hmm... I'm not sure what you're talking about. But in terms of religion, I have the urge to destroy civilizations and races that believe in Gautama Buddha, Jesus Christ, Socrates, and others. We can still use some aspects of Confucius, so I am currently bringing him back.

The relationship with Yaidron, a space being from Planet Elder

D

I recently heard that aliens from Cygnus are intervening in Xi Jinping's China. Are you not from Cygnus?

XI JINPING'S G.S.

We are still fighting in Cygnus, too.

D

Similar to what's happening on Earth?

XI JINPING'S G.S.

Yes. We are still fighting battles in a few places.

D

Is that so?

XI JINPING'S G.S.

Cygnus is one of them.

A

Your forces were overwhelmed during the battles in Andromeda Galaxy and Planet Zeta (Magellanic Clouds) and escaped, correct?

XI JINPING'S G.S.

I wouldn't say "escaped," but it may have been because we could not adapt.

A

What do you think are your chances of winning on Earth?

XI JINPING'S G.S.

Huh? Our win is almost guaranteed. This is the final game day. What did you think?

A

So, you think here is the final game?

XI JINPING'S G.S.

The world emperor will soon be decided.

A

But Yaidron, who is a space being and a god of justice-like being, told us...

XI JINPING'S G.S.

Ah, him. That Yaidron was our enemy on Zeta.

A

So, he's your enemy.

XI JINPING'S G.S.

Yaidron from Planet Elder drove us out.

A

I see.

"I have been working to conciliate Europe and drag Obama into the mess"

A

Yaidron said that even if China were to beat the U.S., they still have to face India and the Islamic regions, so there are a few more stages to clear... (See *With Savior: Messages from Space Being Yaidron* [Tokyo: HS Press, 2020].)

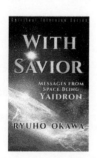

XI JINPING'S G.S.

They are tenacious, so that may be true. That is why we are trying to destroy India before they become a hegemonic nation.

A

Trying to destroy them?

XI JINPING'S G.S.

Yes. We are trying to.

A

But thinking from a strategic standpoint, even in terms of China's tactics, fighting opponents simultaneously on all sides is...

XI JINPING'S G.S.

It would be difficult to accomplish this without a considerable amount of super power. Since I assumed my position as president, I have been working to conciliate Europe and drag Obama into the mess. Trump was the only one who tried to oppose, but because the U.S. preferred mobocracy, he was destroyed. Soon, he will either go to prison or be exiled abroad. We have many enemies.

Additionally, Europe is being brought to ruin. We'll first break the U.K. away from Europe and then destroy it. After that, as for Europe, its center is Germany, but they unfortunately lost WWII, so we will...

The one who infiltrated Germany back then was not us, but another one of our allies.

B

Who would that be?

XI JINPING'S G.S.

I shouldn't say too much about others.

A

Others?

XI JINPING'S G.S.

The ones that were here during the age of Atlantis.

A

Do you know any specific names?

XI JINPING'S G.S.

They are different from us, so I cannot say.

"We destroyed the red race that prospered in the ancient American civilization"

A

I think the U.S. presidential election was greatly affected by the way Americans thought. We learned that when people are soaked with left-wing thinking, materialistic views, or pro-totalitarianism ideas held by GAFA and others, they are quite easily taken advantage of.

XI JINPING'S G.S.

We have many options. This is actually the second time we destroy the American civilization.

A

The second time?

XI JINPING'S G.S.

Yes. We destroyed it once.

B

So, you also took part in destroying it the first time?

XI JINPING'S G.S.

There used to be a red race in America, and there was a period when its civilization flourished, but it was almost completely annihilated. Some of these red people regressed to a primitive life and survived as Native Americans. Nearly all of them perished.

We waged war using atomic bombs. When was that? Hmm... it was not as far back as 2,000 years ago, but more than 1,000 years ago, maybe around second, third, or fourth century A.D. (Author's Note: The exact time period is yet to be determined through a spiritual reading.) The civilization was rooted out. The center of the civilization was in the Nevada desert today. It has turned into a desert.

B

According to one source, it was an attack from Mars.

XI JINPING'S G.S.

There were others. It is unlikely that I did nothing before I came to Earth. I built a frontline base on Mars before I came to Earth. So, I have forces on Mars, too.

B

I see.

"In pragmatism and scientific technology, we surpassed the earthlings, but lost because of religion"

A

You said that you were defeated by a god that teaches love, mercy, and self-reflection, at least in Andromeda.

XI JINPING'S G.S.

It was not like that in Andromeda. We were actually similar to each other in a sense.

A

Similar to your way of thinking?

XI JINPING'S G.S.

It was like a battle of *bushido* (samurai spirit).

A

A battle of *bushido*?

XI JINPING'S G.S.

I think it was "*bushido* vs. *bushido*."

B

Was it really *Bushido* [*smiles wryly*]?

A

So, what you mean is that only the strong should win.

XI JINPING'S G.S.

It was like a battle between the old Japanese schools of swordsmanship.

B

But one of the virtues of *bushido* is to help the weak.

XI JINPING'S G.S.

I don't know. I don't care.

B

Bushido is not to destroy the weak, but to help them.

XI JINPING'S G.S.

I don't care. It is basically about defeating one's opponent.

A

It must include the virtue of protecting the value of something holy.

XI JINPING'S G.S.
Hmm. I don't know.

A
You don't know?

XI JINPING'S G.S.
I don't know, but in Andromeda...

A
You did say that those who talk about love are weak.

XI JINPING'S G.S.
They are.

A
Then why is it that you were defeated?

XI JINPING'S G.S.

They were weak. Their country declined because it was weak.

A

They declined, but why were you expelled or why did you flee from Andromeda?

XI JINPING'S G.S.

They just surpassed us in armed forces.

A

So, their armed forces were stronger?

XI JINPING'S G.S.

Yes. Now we are also doing something that is going against our values. We let the U.S. form a "merciful" government. It will end up destroying the U.S.

A

But there is no mercy in you.

XI JINPING'S G.S.

No, there isn't.

A

No.

XI JINPING'S G.S.

None.

A

In Earth's history, the Yuan dynasty sent its military forces into Europe, but in the end, it did not win. Why was that?

XI JINPING'S G.S.

That's because Christian culture and Islamic culture were already strong. In fact, we surpassed them in terms of pragmatism in your terms, and also scientific technology, but we could not establish something like religion, as earthlings did. I think that was the reason for our defeat.

A

I see. You mean, religion has something to do with strength.

XI JINPING'S G.S.

No, religion is connected with weakness.

A

But you just said that not being able to create one was the cause of your defeat.

XI JINPING'S G.S.

The weak turn to religion for help. So, we don't need it. Our leader had to be a genius to keep us strong, so we could not always sustain our dynasty by bloodline.

B

So, you are saying the Yuan dynasty couldn't last because you couldn't leave behind a basic philosophy.

XI JINPING'S G.S.

Exactly. We couldn't leave any philosophy behind.

We were advanced in scientific technology, rather than pragmatism.

Will Europe, the U.S., Asia, and Africa bow down to the "World Emperor" Xi Jinping?

A

That means current China will follow the footsteps of the Yuan Dynasty.

XI JINPING'S G.S.

Well, you have a point there. But I'll become the world emperor before that. So, I am considering exporting the "Xi Jinping Thought" to the world.

C

When will you be able to call yourself the world emperor?

XI JINPING'S G.S.

When the U.S. president comes to Beijing to show loyalty to us. I think Japan will soon do so and visit us again. When European countries depend on China for financial support. When African and Asian countries live by relying on China's mercy. Also, when Great Britain apologizes to the world for its past invasion, saying that they were similar to Hitler in nature. Once we achieve these situations, I can be the world emperor.

Japan isn't counted in the picture. I am thinking about using it as a servant.

A

You aim to achieve that far?

XI JINPING'S G.S.

Yes.

"Christianity is already a puppet when it comes to matters involving China"

A

Now religion is declining all over the world. People's faith has weakened around the world.

XI JINPING'S G.S.

Exactly.

A

You can take the advantage of this situation to infiltrate into other countries. But what if a new religion emerges and the next generation starts to gain strong faith?

XI JINPING'S G.S.

There is no point in answering such a hypothetical question [*laughs*].

A

Do you think it's unlikely?

XI JINPING'S G.S.

Look at the situation in Hong Kong. The chief executive of Hong Kong is a Christian, and Agnes Chow and the guy...

C

Joshua Wong.

XI JINPING'S G.S.

Joshua Wong. I remember they are also Christians. Christians are fighting against each other, and one side has sent the other side to jail. It's been long since Christianity ceased to be the philosophy of love, and became the philosophy of division [*laughs*]. It's already a philosophy of division and confrontation. It has become meaningless.

In China, there is a confrontation between underground churches and aboveground churches. Both of them are already under the surveillance of Chinese authorities. It's just a matter of which hand we put them on. We now have the right to appoint the bishops of Christian churches in our country. Christianity is already a puppet when it comes to matters involving China. So it's over.

8

What Is the "Xi Jinping Thought" Regarding China?

"In China, those who stand against me cannot survive"

B

We have heard you speak about the Xi Jinping Thought, mainly regarding countries around the world. Now we would like to talk about the domestic issues in China.

According to the announcement released by the Chinese government, and other data and research sources, the recent flood has left tens of millions to a hundred million people homeless.

XI JINPING'S G.S.

They don't need houses. They used to live in caves.

B

According to the Xi Jinping Thought, are you saying that they should live in caves?

XI JINPING'S G.S.

Even Xi Jinping himself once lived in a cave when he was sent to the countryside.

B

Right.

The reason why people lost their homes is because the authorities gave the order to destroy the levee upstream and drown the people who lived there, in order to protect the wealthy privileged class who lived downstream. We've heard a lot that China had no bones about doing such things. Is this one of the applications of your idea of "being strong justifies everything"?

XI JINPING'S G.S.

In China, those who stand against Beijing, or namely me, cannot survive. I won't even allow them to flee abroad. I will just kill them.

B

I see. So, you have no qualms about breaking the levee.

Alien-human hybrid experiments in Inner Mongolia, Uyghur region, and Tibet

XI JINPING'S G.S.

We can increase the population as much as we want. Regarding Inner Mongolia, Uyghur Autonomous Region, and Tibet, you, Happy Science, criticize me for doing similar things as Hitler, but you are wrong. I am doing more than what Hitler did.

A

More than Hitler.

XI JINPING'S G.S.

You are all idiots.

A

I see...

XI JINPING'S G.S.

We are conducting alien-human hybrid experiments. The Han Chinese are too precious to experiment with, so we are using those "inferior" people to crossbreed them with aliens.

B

Let me ask you a question regarding this.

XI JINPING'S G.S.

We can increase the population as much as we want. So, whether it's a flood or a plague of locusts, I don't mind if people die. We can increase the population to make up for the loss. We ended our one-child policy on the premise that people die.

B

In our recent issue of *The Liberty*, we wrote an article about man-made soldiers being produced as an early stage of those experiments.

XI JINPING'S G.S.

You have written the article as if you have seen this.

B

It's almost as credible as if we did.

"China researches body modification so that aliens can immigrate to Earth"

B

Judging from various spiritual messages in the past, it is obvious that you are thinking or planning to modify human bodies so that aliens or their souls can immigrate to China, or Earth.

XI JINPING'S G.S.

Exactly. There are many aliens waiting to be earthlings.

B

You explain to your people that body modification is necessary to create super soldiers, but you are actually modifying the bodies for future immigrated aliens.

XI JINPING'S G.S.

Exactly. We are working on it.

B

I thought so. OK.

XI JINPING'S G.S.

We are researching it. Hitler started the experiment, but he couldn't go so far.

Our souls can "walk-in" on human bodies, but we need to modify the body so that our souls can directly control it or become a master of it. We can't do so as it is now.

"We need a body that can survive in hotter and colder temperatures"

A

This is really interesting. What characteristics does the body of space people from your planet have? You are thinking about crossbreeding humans with them, aren't you?

XI JINPING'S G.S.

Well... we need to create a body that is able to survive in a little hotter temperature and...

A

A hotter temperature?

XI JINPING'S G.S.

And in a colder temperature as well.

A

You mean, you literally have thick skin. What do you really look like?

XI JINPING'S G.S.

Human bodies are too fragile for us. We cannot survive with such soft, thin skin of yours.

A

Can you stand on two legs?

XI JINPING'S G.S.

We can. Yes.

A

You can?

XI JINPING'S G.S.

Yes.

A

And you are as tall as us.

XI JINPING'S G.S.

Actually, we need to adjust the size of the body because we are short on food.

"People in the occupied territories will be modified first, and the ruling class later"

XI JINPING'S G.S.

Also… It's easy to enter the body of Chinese people because they eat anything from reptiles to amphibians. They even eat bats. Or, maybe not? I don't know. Compared to other countries, they eat anything.

India has such a huge population, but they don't eat animals very much to get protein, so they are all skinny. They are skinny because they only eat curry.

B

One of the *Star Wars* movies depicts that the man-made soldiers or cloned soldiers, who used to be obedient, suddenly become rebellious to ruling members upon receiving a single order, and take over the entire empire. Do you suspect such a future may come?

XI JINPING'S G.S.
No, that will not happen. The CCP members amount to about 90 million, and they have been trained to control 1.4 billion people. We are making a philosophy to make sure that the ruling structure will not change. After witnessing how the U.S. was defeated, we are now working hard to enlighten our people about how fragile two-party parliamentary democracy is.

B
So, the CCP members in the future will be... I shouldn't say "monsters," but those with a modified body?

XI JINPING'S G.S.
No, we won't do that from the start. We will start by modifying the bodies of people in the occupied regions to make them soldiers.

B
I see.

XI JINPING'S G.S.
First, we will transform them into strong soldiers. It is a little risky to conduct a crossbreeding on the ruling class, so we will do that later.

B
I see.

"If the different ethnic groups try to gain independence, China will break up into 17 regions"

A
Last summer, Master Okawa had a dream of a huge winged-dragon with 17 heads and tails going on a rampage. Do you have any idea what this huge dragon might be?

XI JINPING'S G.S.
Hmm... Well, we might have 17 heads.

A

You might?

XI JINPING'S G.S.

Yes. We have many ethnic groups under our control, but if they were to fight for independence, China will break up into about 17 "heads" or regions. China is made up of many different races. The Han people now keep other ethnic groups under control, but there are many of them, so if they were to gain independence, China might well dissolve into separate regions.

You accuse us of Inner Mongolia and Uyghur region issues, but if these people should succeed in gaining independence, other ethnic groups would also try to become independent. You don't know China. You may think Chinese people are all Han race, but they are not. All races will start to seek independence.

The period during which the Han people ruled the country was very short. Even the Tang dynasty which you may consider the most famous era of Chinese history was not actually ruled by the Han race. It was the Xianbei people. China has been ruled by various ethnic groups. The Yuan dynasty was governed by the Mongols, while the

Qing dynasty by the Manchu. So, the ethnic groups... The Jin dynasty was not ruled by the Chinese, either. Jin, Jin, Jin, Jin... Jin (Later Jin) was during the Ming dynasty, but they were not Hans, either.

So, China has been ruled by different ethnic groups. If you count all of them, it will probably amount to about 17. And before that, ethnic groups intruded into China from the Turkish region, or Central Asia, from Russia, Afghanistan, Middle East, India, and North and South Korea. Even Taiwan was once a pirate country.

A
So, you are bringing together all the ethnic groups.

XI JINPING'S G.S.
The CCP now controls them and China is enjoying a very happy period. It has become the strongest country in the world and unified through one ideology, you know?

Dongting Lake Niangniang is trying to bring about the "Water Revolution" in China

C

Happy Science has been receiving messages from the spirit world, and since last year, a spirit called Dongting Lake Niangniang has appeared.

XI JINPING'S G.S.

[*Clicks tongue.*] Do you want me to bury the (Dongting) lake?

C

There is a key phrase, the "Water Revolution" (see p.212).

XI JINPING'S G.S.

Keep saying that, and I will bury the lake.

C

I think that you know there is such a movement in the spirit world. It means that the power of the spirit world is at work to bring about a revolution to change the Chinese regime.

XI JINPING'S G.S.

Insurgence. It is like an insurgent group. If you keep pushing the Dongting Lake, I will really bury it.

A

It is not an insurgent group. If you value Confucius, you probably know the legendary leaders such as Yao, Shun, and Yu. Dongting Lake Niangniang was a daughter of Yao.

XI JINPING'S G.S.

I don't know. I don't care.

A

Dongting Lake Niangniang is a rightful being in the Chinese history.

XI JINPING'S G.S.

It's just an old legend. Their dynasty was as small as a village. It's completely different from the current modernized China, which has conquered the world and has the ability to launch rockets into space and collect the researched data.

A

However, ancient China was founded by politicians such as Yao, Shun, and Yu who believed in Shangdi.

XI JINPING'S G.S.
Hmm.

A

It began from there.

XI JINPING'S G.S.
But they are ancient people. It was something like the ancient Native Americans that believed in their god. Seeing from today's China that is trying to control the universe, it is such a primitive era from a long time ago [*laughs*].

A

But the spiritual power...

XI JINPING'S G.S.
Dongting Lake Niangniang is probably just a huge eel or something living in the lake.

A

But you actually suffered from last year's flood.

XI JINPING'S G.S.

When a river overflows, it does sometimes look like a dragon.

A

Why do you think you suffered from it?

XI JINPING'S G.S.

I don't know.

A

That was not just a physical event, but...

XI JINPING'S G.S.

Ah, there are things I don't know, of course. But even if 100 million Chinese people die, we just need to modify the human body, so I don't mind.

A

I see.

"We cooperated with Qin Shi Huang, and only used Mao Zedong"

A

What is your spiritual connection to Qin Shi Huang?

XI JINPING'S G.S.

Who?

A

Qin Shi Huang.

XI JINPING'S G.S.

Oh, Qin Shi Huang... It was not us who influenced Qin Shi Huang, but other beings granted him wisdom.

A

It was not you?

XI JINPING'S G.S.

Well, it was not exactly us who helped him, but we are now working together with them.

A

Working together?

XI JINPING'S G.S.

Yes. Working together.

A

What has become of your connection with Mao Zedong now?

XI JINPING'S G.S.

We just used him.

A

Used him?

XI JINPING'S G.S.

Mao Zedong was weak, so he was likely to be defeated. The Japanese Army was fighting the troops led by Chiang Kai-shek. The Communist Party led by Mao Zedong fled further and further to the west. Like Liu Bei of Shu from *The Records of the Three Kingdoms*, he fled from the

Japanese Army, going deep into the mountains and moving from cave to cave.

The Japanese Army weakened the Chiang Kai-shek troops, but because it was defeated in the end, the Communist Party was able to win the civil war and Mao could make a comeback.

I didn't expect Mao to become a ruler in China. But thanks to the fierce attack of the U.S., Japan was defeated. If Japan hadn't been defeated, there wouldn't have been the Mao Zedong regime.

A

I see. Does it mean that the weight of spiritual power shifted in China?

XI JINPING'S G.S.

Well, I had never thought that Mao would become so strong, but I did use him.

The power relationship between
Mr. Xi Jinping and Ahriman

A

Let me get back to the topic of Ahriman. What exactly is
your relationship with Ahriman?

XI JINPING'S G.S.

Umm... Ahriman is my minion.

A

Your minion?

XI JINPING'S G.S.

Yes.

A

Since when exactly has he become your minion? Was
it recent?

XI JINPING'S G.S.

Hmm...

A

Or was he originally your minion?

XI JINPING'S G.S.

Zoroastrianism made its way into China.

A

Yes.

XI JINPING'S G.S.

A long time ago. Zoroastrianism made its way in as fire worship, and umm... I was taking care of that, too.

Hmm, Ahriman... Ahriman... Ahriman... We destroyed Zoroaster in this world, but next... Well, religions emerge one after another in the Middle East. When a new religion is born, an old one is destroyed, so I don't quite know about the details. But Zoroastrianism is still surviving even now.

Hmm... Hmm... Ahriman. Where was he? He appeared in various places quite often. When Pol Pot killed about two million people in Cambodia, I think Ahriman was there. He is not always in China.

A

He is your minion, but does his superior change so often?

XI JINPING'S G.S.

Well... There are a lot of "bosses." Yes, bosses.

A

OK. Do you know that Ahriman comes from the flip-side universe?

XI JINPING'S G.S.

He might, but there are a lot of bosses, and there must be the head of those bosses.

A

Is there a head?

XI JINPING'S G.S.

Yes.

A

Is that you?

XI JINPING'S G.S.
Yes. Now that Xi Jinping is in a position to become the world emperor, the head has become one with Xi Jinping.

"The inventor of dark matter is the primordial god of the universe"

A
But there is an entity that you worship as god, right?

XI JINPING'S G.S.
Huh?

A
The one above the head of the bosses.

XI JINPING'S G.S.
What I consider god? There is no such thing on Earth.

A
How about in the universe?

XI JINPING'S G.S.

Yes. There is a stronger one in the universe.

B

Stronger than you?

XI JINPING'S G.S.

Yes.

B

Oh. Who exactly is that?

XI JINPING'S G.S.

I don't know. It's beyond me. I don't know, but there is one that created the darkness of the universe. So, he is the creator who created darkness.

There is a being who invented dark matter. He is the real primordial god of the universe. The one who raised a rebellion against him was the god of light, the one at the root of Ahura Mazda.

A

Rebellion...

XI JINPING'S G.S.

Yes. The universe is darkness.

A

You mean there is a philosophy that the universe is darkness?

XI JINPING'S G.S.

No, it is not a philosophy, but the universe is essentially darkness.

A

Do you know who created the universe?

XI JINPING'S G.S.

Umm, he is like a coal tar... He is millions of light-years away, so I don't know. But he does exist.

You have now discovered black holes, and I think he is on the other side of the black hole. When a star dies, it turns into a black hole, right? If planet Earth shrinks to about 1.77 cm in diameter, it will turn into a black hole. This black hole will then absorb all other things in the solar system. When this happens, where would they go? They go to what we call the flip-side universe.

A

OK. So, the one you consider god exists there?

XI JINPING'S G.S.

Yes. The flip-side universe is in fact the main body of the universe. What is seen outside is just a small part of this flip-side universe. The absorbed part, and the surrounding area, is the vast universe you call the flip-side universe.

A

Ahriman isn't the master there, is he?

XI JINPING'S G.S.

No, he is just a minion.

A

A minion.

XI JINPING'S G.S.

Hmm. A minion. Yes.

A

Ah, it's my first time hearing that.

9

How to Dominate the World with the Xi Jinping Thought

"I hate democracy. I can't believe in the idea that humans have Buddha-nature"

A

The story has become too grand in scale, so let me get back to our times. What do you think the future holds for Earth? What do you want to do with it?

XI JINPING'S G.S.

You know, umm... Well, I hate democracy. I can't believe in the idea that humans have Buddha-nature or that they are children of God. The universe is made up of dark matter. It is the monism of darkness.

A

You mean, humans are innately evil?

XI JINPING'S G.S.

The monism of absolute darkness. There is no evil, and what you consider evil is an illusion.

A

What is the relation between materialism and the monism of darkness?

XI JINPING'S G.S.

Materialism is... Your thought focuses on this galaxy and this solar system, which contain planets and celestial bodies that are like tiny spots in the darkness. We are beings that are looking at those things from the outside, far away.

You are thinking that I am not speaking straight to the point, aren't you?

B

No, no. What is embracing all of that is actually light.

XI JINPING'S G.S.

No, it is darkness. What are you talking about?

B

Now, I understand clearly that things look completely opposite depending on the angle from which they are viewed.

XI JINPING'S G.S.

I will annihilate whoever revolts against me. The coronavirus symbolizes this. In other words, I will annihilate all those who turn against me.

"I will liberate Japan from American colonialism and make it pay tribute to China"

C

Let me ask you more specific questions. We mentioned earlier the spiritual dream in which a 17-headed dragon was being violent. This can be interpreted as some possible invasion toward Japan in the near future. Is there any plot you are contriving against Japan?

XI JINPING'S G.S.

What are you talking about? We are trying to liberate Japan. Japan has been the colony of the U.S. Do you know that? Japan has been under the colonial rule of the U.S. for more than 70 years. It is still a colony of the U.S. Do you know how many U.S. military bases there are in Japan? You say that Japan is protected by the U.S., but it is actually ruled by the U.S. You live as slaves under the colonial rule of the U.S.

You were originally under the control of China, so paying tribute to China is the proper attitude Japan should have. I am trying to liberate Japan from the colonial rule of the U.S. The day will come when you are liberated, so look forward to it. The day will soon come when all Japanese people offer gratitude to Chinese people every morning for allowing them to use Chinese characters, which they had "stolen" from China.

C

"Soon" means you are planning concrete actions?

XI JINPING'S G.S.

Yes. We just need to kick the U.S. out of Japan. That's it. I will create a situation in which the U.S. has to withdraw.

B

Could you tell us specifically what you mean by "having to withdraw"?

XI JINPING'S G.S.

Mr. Biden will be awarded the Nobel Peace Prize and will reduce the U.S. troops in Japan, resulting in American isolationism as Mr. Trump advocated. Unfortunately for you, it's true. They appeared to have expressed different things, but the conclusion will be the same.

B

I see.

The strategy to dominate the polytheistic India

B

As we look at the events of this year and the next, the Winter Olympics in Beijing is expected to be held next year. Because China is the host country, some countries have called for a boycott of the Olympics. This trend may spread around the world.

If you decide to take some military actions against Taiwan, I'm sure there will be fierce backlash from the international society. Do you still think you can successfully overcome the issue by simply forcing your idea?

XI JINPING'S G.S.

You are a fool. You are not very smart, are you? I've told you Japan belongs to China. You should be worrying about Japan rather than Taiwan!

B

But I think Japan and Taiwan share a common destiny. And if I dare respond to your comment just now, I believe Japan has responsibilities as a former colonial master and it must think about protecting Taiwan. That's why I am asking this question.

XI JINPING'S G.S.

In addition, we need to turn India into a materialistic country. Otherwise, we won't be able to rule over it.

India is based on polytheism and worships too many gods. It's very annoying. Polytheism is a primitive religion. India needs to be wiped clean. Ideologically, we need to turn India into a complete materialist and abolish all its religions. Then, we will inject the new Xi Jinping Thought and redevelop the country under Chinese capital.

B

Could you give me some specific examples of how you are planning to bring materialistic ideology into India?

XI JINPING'S G.S.

First, we must abolish religions. We need to destroy everything.

About the "zero CO₂" pledge

XI JINPING'S G.S.

In any case, why don't you just focus on reducing CO_2 as much as possible? Oil fields are ours. We'll take over all the oil fields.

B

I was hoping to hear you say that because we are dealing with this matter in the next issue of *The Liberty* magazine. China officially pledged to achieve zero CO_2 emissions by 2060.

XI JINPING'S G.S.

Ha [*laughs*]! We have never kept our pledges anyway.

B

You never keep your promises?

XI JINPING'S G.S.

No, we never keep our promises. I just want other countries to keep their promises.

B

So, those are the words from you, the guardian of China.

XI JINPING'S G.S.

Well, we don't want CO_2 emissions from coal anymore because it damages our respiratory system unless we wear masks. So, I want to use a more efficient fuel. Just switching from coal to oil will help us a great deal indeed.

"The Xi Jinping Thought now" means devouring all resources

B

If so, you have every intention to expand your reach toward the oil regions, or invade and rule such areas.

XI JINPING'S G.S.

We have to take Indonesia, too.

B

I see, Indonesia.

XI JINPING'S G.S.

And Brunei. We have to take that, too. I also want to go after the North Sea oil fields in Europe. You know the oil fields that caused England's Brexit? I am hoping to take those too.

B

How about Iran?

XI JINPING'S G.S.

Well, they are approaching China now. So, very soon, we will "prey" on them. To protect themselves from the U.S., they have no choice but to come under our wing.

B

In that case, with regard to the sea lanes...

XI JINPING'S G.S.

China will seize all the oil and natural gas. Your job is to increase the number of countries that will work to reduce CO_2 emissions.

B

Then, it must be imperative for you to put Taiwan under your ruling. It seems to be your next logical move.

XI JINPING'S G.S.

Actually, Taiwan is just a small stepping-stone to cross the river. It's just one of the stones. It's not worth my attention [*laughs*].

My eyes are on Australia's coal and iron ore, Brunei's oil fields, and North Sea oil fields. Also, Iran, Iraq, and Saudi Arabia with their oil fields. I am going after all of them. I want to enslave Africa again. It will be a good location for making human clones. So, I am interested in Africa, too.

B

So, "the Xi Jinping Thought now" means devouring all resources around the world.

"We will swallow up GAFA and make China's internet rule the world"

XI JINPING'S G.S.

Right now, 90 million people of the CCP control 1.4 billion Chinese. My next plan is to have these 1.4 billion people control 7.8 billion people of the world. Actually, about 100 million people will die soon (of coronavirus, etc.), so we will be ruling over 7.7 billion people.

B

You have mentioned "enslavement" just a little while ago. Does this mean a portion of the Chinese people will enslave other human beings?

XI JINPING'S G.S.

Overseas Chinese people are quite successful already. While Jewish people just wandered around the world, Chinese capital is taking over the world financially. Jewish capital is getting kicked out from the U.S. and being replaced by the Chinese capital. The American media used to be under Jewish capital, but Chinese capital is beginning to dominate them now.

In other words, the world belongs to China. One way to do this is by taking control of the energy source. Other countries should just focus on moving away from fossil fuels and switching to solar, wind, and other clean energy that will not emit CO_2. In the meantime, we will take over fossil fuels.

Another way is by conquering the internet. We will soon swallow up GAFA. I will let GAFA be sucked into a "black hole" and make Chinese internet rule the world. This is our next strategy. It's part of the Xi Jinping Thought.

B

So that's clearly part of your strategy.

XI JINPING'S G.S.

It's the Xi Jinping Thought. We'll accomplish the opposite of what Trump had tried to do.

B

It was certainly evident from the current state of affairs.

XI JINPING'S G.S.

Yes, indeed.

B

The statement you just made is in fact important evidence.

The truth about GAFA's record profits during the coronavirus pandemic

XI JINPING'S G.S.

The U.S. couldn't win. They claimed that the People's Liberation Army was behind the scenes and tried to remove all Chinese-related internet services, but they couldn't beat us in the end. It is time for them to be swallowed up by us.

GAFA and everyone else are desperate to get into our 1.4 billion market. They will ultimately surrender for the sake of profits. They are reporting record high profits, you know? They are being bought by us already.

B

So, GAFA have the desires to get profit and are falling for it. Is that what you are saying?

XI JINPING'S G.S.

Right. This is a bribe, but since they are not politicians,

it is not illegal. If the politicians took bribes, it would be a crime, though.

GAFA made the highest profit ever, right?

B
Their highest profit is due to...

XI JINPING'S G.S.
During the coronavirus pandemic, GAFA reported record high profits. When solving a murder mystery, you just need to find out who profited from the murder.

B
In short, you let them gain more profits than they usually do.

XI JINPING'S G.S.
They profited a lot, right?

B
Yes. Was that your doing behind the scenes?

XI JINPING'S G.S.

GAFA earned the highest profits ever in their history by taking advantage of the situation where 400,000 Americans were dying (at the time of this spiritual message).

B

You just pointed out something that Americans themselves haven't realized yet.

XI JINPING'S G.S.

Yes. They will all be under Chinese control very soon. The time is near. Thanks to Biden.

"Chinese vaccine contains something that can mutate humans"

XI JINPING'S G.S.

Whether to cure Biden's dementia or worsen it is in our hands. You should know that we also have control of American medical institutions.

B

We do know that already. I am intentionally staying away from the topic.

XI JINPING'S G.S.

We also excel in the field of medicine. We are experts. Medicine is materialism, after all.

B

I see. Now, I am hesitant to ask these questions I have.

XI JINPING'S G.S.

Hold on. You tend to draw your own conclusions too quickly. So, let me give you more explanations.

B

[*Laughs.*] OK.

XI JINPING'S G.S.

Relating to the topic of GAFA earlier, we are also strong in the field of medicine. Many different vaccines have now been produced. But you should all be careful of what is in those vaccines because they could contain something extra, and this extra something could control you. Be warned.

B

Yes, OK.

XI JINPING'S G.S.

Now you may ask your next questions.

B

Thank you very much. In fact, you have already answered one of my two questions.

Many Japanese people are afraid that the current vaccines developed by the Western nations are not going to be effective and China's versions will circulate next.

XI JINPING'S G.S.

We overcame the coronavirus, you know? Do you want to know why Chinese people didn't die? That's because the Chinese already had vaccines for the virus [*laughs*]. By the time this pandemic began, we had already completed producing vaccines.

Ultimately, you will learn that none of the Western vaccines work. It is effective for a little while, but it won't work against the new strain. Then, a new vaccine will need to be developed for it, so everyone will eventually look to China and ask for our vaccines.

Chinese vaccines have something in them that could mutate human beings. If you take those, you will be controlled by us. Then, more people will become part of the Chinese race.

We have advanced this far. We are already on a different level. We are much smarter up here [*points to his head*] than you are. You should know that the University of Tokyo is already no match for Tsinghua University.

B

Umm, OK. I understand that the Chinese vaccines contain some kind of a brainwashing effect.

XI JINPING'S G.S.

You should all go get those American and British vaccines. They won't work anyway. In the end, everyone will come to rely on the Chinese vaccine. Indian vaccines are out of the question; people wouldn't want theirs even for free. Then, people will end up relying on Chinese vaccines and before long, they will turn into Chinese without their noticing.

B

Thank you for your answers. Actually, our next issue features articles on the ineffectiveness of the coronavirus vaccines [*laughs*].

10

Xi Jinping's Guardian Spirit Is Aiming at "Cleaning Out" Earth

"We abduct Americans and modify their bodies"

B

I have another question regarding a similar issue. We've heard that you already reached largely into the U.S. pharmaceutical industry and other medical fields as well.

XI JINPING'S G.S.

That's right.

B

This has actually been obvious based on the circumstantial evidence.

We learned that alien walk-ins have been taking place for the central figures in China (see *Zoroaster – Uchu no Yami no Kami to Dou Tatakau-ka* – [lit., "Zoroaster – How to Fight the God of Darkness of the Universe –"] and *R. A. Goal – Chikyu no Mirai o Hiraku Kotoba* – [lit., "R.

A. Goal – Words to Open Earth's Future –"]). In the same way, is there any possibility that those in medicine and other related fields in the U.S., for example, have also been bought off, or even under some kind of influence, including a spiritual one?

XI JINPING'S G.S.

Well, I don't want to answer that question, because I would be revealing too much information.

In fact, there are several types, so it's not just one kind. There are others, too.

We have been making inroads from Canada and the region around Alaska. Yes. We are not approaching the mainland U.S. directly, but invading largely through those areas.

In the U.S., we are mainly abducting people and modifying their bodies. Things don't go as we planned with the Americans because they are stubborn. So, we abduct them and modify their bodies. Just like salmons that were investigated, we tag them and set them free.

The estimated American abductees must have already reached around 10 million. That's our... I mean, about 10 million people act as a result of receiving transmitted signals from us, even though they may believe they are acting of their own free will. We intend to gradually increase the number of such people.

B

Yes, we've also heard that a kind of chip has been implanted in some people.

XI JINPING'S G.S.

That's right as far as the U.S. is concerned.

As for Canada and Alaska, we now have a little different version of the invasion plan.

B

Ah. Does a "different version" also involve some kind of body modification?

XI JINPING'S G.S.

No, people around there are a little weaker.

Those in the mainland U.S. are somewhat difficult to brainwash because they have a very rigid way of thinking. So, we need to add some modifications to their bodies. But we can easily go into places like Canada and Alaska.

B

Oh, I see. So, you have already been in those areas.

XI JINPING'S G.S.

Yes, we have.

B

I understand.

XI JINPING'S G.S.

We are also aiming at Australia, but Australia is a little... hmm.

B

The prime minister is working hard to resist quite strongly.

XI JINPING'S G.S.

Well, hmm... I think he senses something. He seems to be sensing something.

B

Yes, he clearly recognizes something.

XI JINPING'S G.S.

Right. He is cautious.

B

Yes, he seems to have relevant information, I mean information related to your doing.

XI JINPING'S G.S.

Hmm... yes, that's true, because there is plenty of underground information.

But anyway, as someone who had held a leading position on Earth many times in the past, we intend to do the same this time, too, to some level.

Predicting how President Biden will handle UFO information

A

Information about UFOs is going to be disclosed in the U.S. and...

XI JINPING'S G.S.

Well, Biden will probably disclose very little.

A

Is there any information that will be inconvenient to you, if disclosed?

XI JINPING'S G.S.

Hmm... Alien technologies can be used in the private sectors once it's made open to public.

A

Are there any technologies—in energy or power-related fields, for example—that will put you in trouble if disclosed?

XI JINPING'S G.S.

Well, disclosing information means other countries can use the technologies for military purposes. We have kept information strictly confidential from each other.

In fact, China doesn't know everything about how many alien technologies have been provided to the U.S.

military forces and the military industry, because they are not the same as what we receive. We don't know how extensively they are provided.

I don't think Biden will disclose important information, but instead sell it to China.

A
Sell?

XI JINPING'S G.S.
He intends to do that.

B
I understand.

"China is now planning to build its base on the dark side of the Moon"

B
You just said, "each other."

XI JINPING'S G.S.
Yes.

B

You said that both the U.S. and China possess some information and hide it from each other, and are speculating the opponent's potential.

XI JINPING'S G.S.

Yes, hmm.

B

At the beginning of this interview, you mentioned that you are provided with various alien technologies. In the past, Master Ryuho Okawa conducted a remote viewing on Area 51 and he said that China is actually provided with the same technologies he found in Area 51.

XI JINPING'S G.S.

Hmm.

B

According to the reading, a time-travel technology is also provided in Area 51. In China, do you have any hidden technologies that were transferred from the aliens, besides the bacteria-related technology?

XI JINPING'S G.S.

Right now, we are planning on building a Chinese base on the dark side of the Moon. The U.S. found that there were already alien bases on the dark side of the Moon, but they were too scared to explore them. After the Apollo program, they got scared and terminated their missions.

But China has made a secret agreement and now intends to build a base on the dark side of the Moon and start interacting with them. We are competing to see who will win in the field of space as well.

B

Does it mean that you have aliens protecting the Chinese space probe as bodyguards on the dark side of the Moon? The U.S. space probe was actually attacked and destroyed, but if a Chinese space probe lands on the Moon, for example...

XI JINPING'S G.S.

We plan to build a base on the Moon and create an alliance in space. I think the U.S. is now trying to colonize Mars, but our plan is to seize the dark side of the Moon first.

"We are trying to rule over the ocean floor as well"

A

In the New Year address, President Xi Jinping said that China has seen breakthroughs in scientific explorations on lunar probe, Mars mission, and deep-sea manned submersible. So, apart from the development on the Moon, have you initiated some plans on Mars and the ocean floor?

XI JINPING'S G.S.

Yes. Well, hmm, the ocean floor represents the boundless future that is still dormant on Earth. So we are now trying to rule over the ocean floor as well. We are thinking about governing it. Other countries are defending their territorial waters above in many ways, but they don't when it comes to the bottom of the sea. So, we have plans to control the ocean floor.

Once we seize the ocean floor, we can obtain abundant oil and minerals that could be used for various industrial resources. We know that abundant mineral resources exist in the seabed that are indispensable to go into outer space.

B

Ah, is that so?

XI JINPING'S G.S.

Hmm.

A

Earlier, you said that the U.S. has plans for Mars.

XI JINPING'S G.S.

So, we are now trying our best to make sure not to let them monopolize Mars. But, well, we don't see that there are a lot of resources on Mars now. It's just the matter of how to deal with the space people who live underground on that planet. (Note: Spiritual readings on Mars conducted in the past reveal the existence of the underground city. Refer to "Kasei Yume Reading – R. A. Goal no Reigen –" [lit. "Reading on a Dream on Mars – A Spiritual Message from R. A. Goal –"] recorded on February 17, 2021, and *UFO Reading II.*)

The reason Happy Science cannot be attacked

B

I have one more question. When you were on the planet Zeta, Yaidron…

XI JINPING'S G.S.

Yes.

B

Yaidron and…

XI JINPING'S G.S.

Ah, that annoying one. He's annoying.

B

Well, and even now, Yaidron and other space beings form a kind of federation, putting Earth under tight security.

XI JINPING'S G.S.

That's right.

B

How do you see...

XI JINPING'S G.S.

We do think of attacking such petty organization as Happy Science all at once. We can easily launch an attack on Happy Science, if we want to. But Yaidron says he has "locked on" to the Chinese Embassy as well, so...

B

Yes.

XI JINPING'S G.S.

So, we'd be in trouble if we were attacked. So I can't do anything.

B

That's the strategy of mutual assured destruction, right?

XI JINPING'S G.S.

Hmm... He (Yaidron) says he'll also give a blow to us and destroy all Chinese facilities.

B

Yes.

"I want to brainwash earthlings with the idea that China is the strongest and the best"

B

Just about a year ago, the space being R. A. Goal also clearly said that should China invade Taiwan, he would threaten it from outer space.

XI JINPING'S G.S.

We don't know which side is more powerful until we actually fight each other. But your side (R. A. Goal and Yaidron) seems to be a little stronger and has a slight advantage now.

In a way, we are in a race of brainwashing the people on Earth. We need to get to the point where more than half of the earthlings support China. For example, when the majority of people on Earth believe that China is the strongest and best country in the world and they want to follow our leadership, I'm afraid they (R. A. Goal and Yaidron) will be kicked out of Earth. We are fighting for this supremacy right now. I will achieve this during my presidency.

B

You want to do it during your presidency.

XI JINPING'S G.S.

Some space beings oppose us, but if earthlings do not support them, they will lose ground on Earth. My goal is to get rid of my enemies (R. A. Goal and Yaidron) from Earth. If I cover this Earth with scientific pragmatism and materialism, and atheist countries, my enemies will have no chance to meddle in Earth's affairs.

C

So, in short, this battle is not only on the level of technology but also on the level of ideas.

XI JINPING'S G.S.

Yes, there is also a battle of ideas because "thinking" is part of human nature.

What's more, I am also considering cleaning out Earth's spiritual world. I think it is about time to reshuffle the spiritual world. There are too many annoying beings. We just need to blow it up.

How do we do it? We can simply strike a large meteorite at Earth. Its destructive energy is so huge that it will even blow up Earth's spirit world.

B

I think blowing up the physical three-dimensional world is a different story from destroying the world of the fourth dimension and above.

XI JINPING'S G.S.

It will blow up for sure—including all those dubious beings.

This is a war of invasion. You haven't been aware that the space invaders war has already begun, but I know.

"After Trump, I want to destroy Happy Science"

A

It is just about time to wrap this up.

XI JINPING'S G.S.

Is that so? Did you understand "the Xi Jinping Thought now"?

A

To conclude this interview, do you have any messages to humankind? Do you want to summarize your future schemes or tell us how you plan to remove obstacles?

XI JINPING'S G.S.

I am trying to start something opposite to what your gods have been saying. We already won one game by defeating Trump. Next, I am going to crush your claim to protect Hong Kong and Taiwan, making Happy Science lose its credibility. It will be certified as a cult, making it difficult for you to live even in Japan. In this way, you will be pushed into a corner within a few years.

A

Does that mean your biggest obstacle in the battle of ideas is Happy Science?

XI JINPING'S G.S.

Hmm... But you will be destroyed by provoking jealousy in Japan anyway. We have identified certain groups in Japan who are jealous of your organization.

A

Now, please give us one last warning, if there is any.

XI JINPING'S G.S.

Hmm.

A

By "us" I mean humans.

XI JINPING'S G.S.

[*About five seconds of silence.*] You know, China is under our complete control. Do not expect to defeat us (China) by mere floods and locusts. Humans can be multiplied endlessly. We are now thinking of multiplying them. New humans will have alien genes incorporated in them, so they will be even stronger. We are making new humans. It is time to clean out Earth.

Our people will increasingly be resistant to any viruses. The rest of the world will continue to suffer from the virus and death tolls will grow larger and larger. You have no other way but to come to us for help. You will be saved when you become Chinese. Hahaha [*laughs*]. That's the conclusion.

A

I understand your points. Thank you very much for sharing your valuable thoughts with us today.

XI JINPING'S G.S.

Very well. You interviewed me politely and remained unusually well-behaved. I commend you for that.

A

Thank you very much.

XI JINPING'S G.S.

So long.

11

After Recording "the Xi Jinping Thought Now"

Xi Jinping's surface consciousness is influenced by a being combined with his guardian spirit

RYUHO OKAWA

[*Claps three times.*] Looking at how the aspect that had never appeared with Xi Jinping's guardian spirit previously has now appeared, I think it's true that he has been walked-in. I think another being is mixed in him. I'm not sure how a walk-in is taking place, but something has probably combined with his guardian spirit and is starting to influence his surface consciousness. That's what it seems like to me. He never talked like this (before).

Well, I suppose Trump's defeat (in the election) was such a "big game" for him. He (Trump) was probably the only person Xi feared a little. But nothing can be done now because people living in this world also play a role.

China was most certainly the largest trading partner (in export) for Japan last year, surpassing the U.S. Japan's top trading partner seems to be alternating between the

U.S. and China. The trade volume between the U.S. and China will probably also grow.

Well, people want to revive the Japanese economy, but if we, Happy Science, oppose China, our opinions will be ignored again, and we might well be pushed to a minority.

Ah [*sighs*]. Well, we must fight back with *The Liberty*. We can only do our best, though our power is still not enough.

[*To interviewer B*] Don't get fired by going to Ginza bars at night. You might be the target of the sneak shot (by the mass media).

B

[*Laughs.*] I definitely won't go.

RYUHO OKAWA

I hope you'd be careful.

Actually, the reporters who are staking out to get sneak shots are also active after 10 p.m., so if their pictures are taken and their identities are revealed, they too, will be forced to resign. But they are like *ninjas* and they never disclose who took the photos.

I think those reporters should also be arrested. They go to Ginza bars as customers at night even during the state of emergency. They too, should be arrested.

[*To interviewers*] You too, watch out. You never know who or where they are targeting. They usually go after a "small target" that is off guard. So, be careful.

First, we must fight a battle of ideas

RYUHO OKAWA

He is becoming increasingly self-confident. I wonder how much we can do. But anyway, let us do our best.

[*To the audience.*] Any questions? Is it OK?

We just had an interview with an open mind, so it is up to each reader to judge it based on his or her own impression. We don't intend to impose any particular ideology. It is fine even if you find it absurd. If you think it is possible, the question is how fearful it is. I think it is at the level even beyond what the Japan Self-Defense Forces are thinking.

The current Japanese administration is probably too preoccupied with other things to consider this issue. Just like Mr. Biden's son, Mr. Suga's son is also in a dangerous situation (over the scandal of entertaining senior officials of the Internal Affairs and Communications Ministry). In these circumstances, Japan could be put under any form of threat. I wonder if this country can truly survive.

I hope everyone will watch out for their steps, and make sure not to trip up.

Well, he (Xi Jinping) can only do things within the span of his own life. Even if he says he can remain the president indefinitely, it's not certain how far he can go. He is eliminating all his potential successors, so we don't know.

Hmm, well, it can't be helped. This is the battle of our times. We must first fight a battle of ideas. We also have other ways to fight.

OK.

A

Thank you very much.

Afterword

When materialism and atheism prevail, the devils' scope of activity also expands. The advancement of scientific thinking alone must not be considered "good."

Every human being not only has the "right" to be happy but also the "duty" to be happy.

Darkness is certainly expanding, but Light is also trying hard to cut through it.

The democratic government of the people, by the people, for the people, is necessary for the current China as well. Not only the people in Hong Kong and Taiwan but also the people in the Uyghur region, Inner Mongolia, and Tibet have the right to pursue freedom, equality, and happiness.

Meanwhile, the reign of terror mainly led by the military has begun in Myanmar (Burma), as well. We must not accept a world that succumbs to violence. It is my hope to make Earth full of love, freedom, and a sense of responsibility.

Ryuho Okawa
Master & CEO of Happy Science Group
March 2, 2021

ABOUT THE AUTHOR

RYUHO OKAWA was born on July 7th 1956, in Tokushima, Japan. After graduating from the University of Tokyo with a law degree, he joined a Tokyo-based trading house. While working at its New York headquarters, he studied international finance at the Graduate Center of the City University of New York. In 1981, he attained Great Enlightenment and became aware that he is El Cantare with a mission to bring salvation to all humankind. In 1986, he established Happy Science. It now has members in over 160 countries across the world, with more than 700 local branches and temples as well as 10,000 missionary houses around the world. The total number of lectures has exceeded 3,250 (of which more than 150 are in English) and over 2,800 books (of which more than 550 are Spiritual Interview Series) have been published, many of which are translated into 31 languages. Many of the books, including *The Laws of the Sun* have become best sellers or million sellers. To date, Happy Science has produced 23 movies. The original story and original concept were given by the Executive Producer Ryuho Okawa. Recent movie titles are *Beautiful Lure–A Modern Tale of "Painted Skin"* (live-action movie scheduled to be released in May 2021), *Yume Handan soshite Kyoufu Taiken e* (literally, "The Interpretation of Dreams and Fearful Experience," live-action movie scheduled to be released in August 2021), and *The Laws of the Universe–The Age of Elohim* (animation movie scheduled to be released in Fall of 2021). He has also composed the lyrics and music of over 400 songs, such as theme songs and featured songs of movies. Moreover, he is the Founder of Happy Science University and Happy Science Academy (Junior and Senior High School), Founder and President of the Happiness Realization Party, Founder and Honorary Headmaster of Happy Science Institute of Government and Management, Founder of IRH Press Co., Ltd., and the Chairperson of New Star Production Co., Ltd. and ARI Production Co., Ltd.

WHAT IS EL CANTARE?

El Cantare means "the Light of the Earth," and is the Supreme God of the Earth who has been guiding humankind since the beginning of Genesis. He is whom Jesus called Father and Muhammad called Allah. Different parts of El Cantare's core consciousness have descended to Earth in the past, once as Alpha and another as Elohim. His branch spirits, such as Shakyamuni Buddha and Hermes, have descended to Earth many times and helped to flourish many civilizations. To unite various religions and to integrate various fields of study in order to build a new civilization on Earth, a part of the core consciousness has descended to Earth as Master Ryuho Okawa.

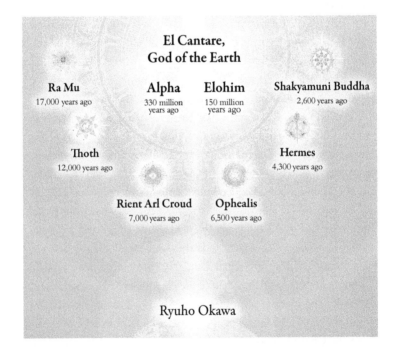

El Cantare,
God of the Earth

Ra Mu	**Alpha**	**Elohim**	**Shakyamuni Buddha**
17,000 years ago	330 million years ago	150 million years ago	2,600 years ago

Thoth	**Hermes**
12,000 years ago	4,300 years ago

Rient Arl Croud	**Ophealis**
7,000 years ago	6,500 years ago

Ryuho Okawa

Alpha is a part of the core consciousness of El Cantare who descended to Earth around 330 million years ago. Alpha preached Earth's Truths to harmonize and unify Earth-born humans and space people who came from other planets.

Elohim is a part of El Cantare's core consciousness who descended to Earth around 150 million years ago. He gave wisdom, mainly on the differences of light and darkness, good and evil.

Shakyamuni Buddha was born as a prince into the Shakya Clan in India around 2,600 years ago. When he was 29 years old, he renounced the world and sought enlightenment. He later attained Great Enlightenment and founded Buddhism.

Hermes is one of the 12 Olympian gods in Greek mythology, but the spiritual Truth is that he taught the teachings of love and progress around 4,300 years ago that became the origin of the current Western civilization. He is a hero that truly existed.

Ophealis was born in Greece around 6,500 years ago and was the leader who took an expedition to as far as Egypt. He is the God of miracles, prosperity, and arts, and is known as Osiris in the Egyptian mythology.

Rient Arl Croud was born as a king of the ancient Incan Empire around 7,000 years ago and taught about the mysteries of the mind. In the heavenly world, he is responsible for the interactions that take place between various planets.

Thoth was an almighty leader who built the golden age of the Atlantic civilization around 12,000 years ago. In the Egyptian mythology, he is known as god Thoth.

Ra Mu was a leader who built the golden age of the civilization of Mu around 17,000 years ago. As a religious leader and a politician, he ruled by uniting religion and politics.

WHAT IS A SPIRITUAL MESSAGE?

We are all spiritual beings living on this earth. The following is the mechanism behind Master Ryuho Okawa's spiritual messages.

1 You are a spirit

People are born into this world to gain wisdom through various experiences and return to the other world when their lives end. We are all spirits and repeat this cycle in order to refine our souls.

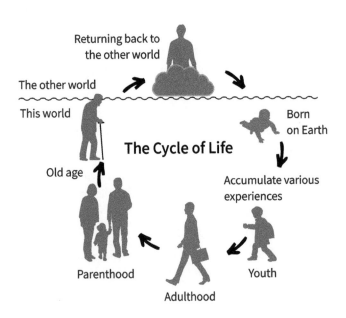

Returning back to
the other world

The other world

This world

Old age

Parenthood

Adulthood

Youth

Born
on Earth

Accumulate various
experiences

The Cycle of Life

2 You have a guardian spirit

Guardian spirits are those who protect the people who are living on this earth. Each of us has a guardian spirit that watches over us and guides us from the other world. They were us in our past life, and are identical in how we think.

3 How spiritual messages work

Master Ryuho Okawa, through his enlightenment, is capable of summoning any spirit from anywhere in the world, including the spirit world.

Master Okawa's way of receiving spiritual messages is fundamentally different from that of other psychic mediums who undergo trances and are thereby completely taken over by the spirits they are channeling.

Master Okawa's attainment of a high level of enlightenment enables him to retain full control of his consciousness and body throughout the duration of the spiritual message. To allow the spirits to express their own thoughts and personalities freely, however, Master Okawa usually softens the dominancy of his consciousness. This way, he is able to keep his own philosophies out of the way and ensure that the spiritual messages are pure expressions of the spirits he is channeling.

Since guardian spirits think at the same subconscious level as the person living on earth, Master Okawa can summon the spirit and find out what the person on earth is actually thinking. If the person has already returned to the other world, the spirit can give messages to the people living on earth through Master Okawa.

Since 2009, more than 1,150 sessions of spiritual messages have been openly recorded by Master Okawa, and the majority of these have been published. Spiritual messages from the guardian spirits of people living today such as Donald Trump, former Japanese Prime Minister Shinzo Abe and Chinese President Xi Jinping, as well as spiritual messages sent from the spirit world by Jesus Christ, Muhammad, Thomas Edison, Mother Teresa, Steve Jobs and Nelson Mandela are just a tiny pack of spiritual messages that were published so far.

Domestically, in Japan, these spiritual messages are being read by a wide range of politicians and mass media, and the high-level contents of these books are delivering an impact even more on politics, news and public opinion. In recent years, there have been spiritual messages recorded in English, and English translations are being done on the spiritual messages given in Japanese. These have been published overseas, one after another, and have started to shake the world.

❶ The guardian spirit / spirit in the other world...

❷ Goes inside Master Okawa in this world

❸ Master Okawa speaks the words of the guardian spirit / spirit

*For more about spiritual messages and a complete list of books in the Spiritual Interview Series, visit **okawabooks.com***

ABOUT HAPPY SCIENCE

Happy Science is a global movement that empowers individuals to find purpose and spiritual happiness and to share that happiness with their families, societies, and the world. With more than 12 million members around the world, Happy Science aims to increase awareness of spiritual truths and expand our capacity for love, compassion, and joy so that together we can create the kind of world we all wish to live in.

Activities at Happy Science are based on the Principles of Happiness (Love, Wisdom, Self-Reflection, and Progress). These principles embrace worldwide philosophies and beliefs, transcending boundaries of culture and religions.

Love teaches us to give ourselves freely without expecting anything in return; it encompasses giving, nurturing, and forgiving.

Wisdom leads us to the insights of spiritual truths, and opens us to the true meaning of life and the will of God (the universe, the highest power, Buddha).

Self-Reflection brings a mindful, nonjudgmental lens to our thoughts and actions to help us find our truest selves—the essence of our souls—and deepen our connection to the highest power. It helps us attain a clean and peaceful mind and leads us to the right life path.

Progress emphasizes the positive, dynamic aspects of our spiritual growth—actions we can take to manifest and spread happiness around the world. It's a path that not only expands our soul growth, but also furthers the collective potential of the world we live in.

PROGRAMS AND EVENTS

The doors of Happy Science are open to all. We offer a variety of programs and events, including self-exploration and self-growth programs, spiritual seminars, meditation and contemplation sessions, study groups, and book events.

Our programs are designed to:
* Deepen your understanding of your purpose and meaning in life
* Improve your relationships and increase your capacity to love unconditionally
* Attain peace of mind, decrease anxiety and stress, and feel positive
* Gain deeper insights and a broader perspective on the world
* Learn how to overcome life's challenges
  ... and much more.

For more information, visit __happy-science.org__.

OUR ACTIVITIES

Happy Science does other various activities to provide support for those in need.

◆ **You Are An Angel! General Incorporated Association**

Happy Science has a volunteer network in Japan that encourages and supports children with disabilities as well as their parents and guardians.

◆ **Never Mind School for Truancy**

At 'Never Mind,' we support students who find it very challenging to attend schools in Japan. We also nurture their self-help spirit and power to rebound against obstacles in life based on Master Okawa's teachings and faith.

◆ **"Prevention Against Suicide" Campaign since 2003**

A nationwide campaign to reduce suicides; over 20,000 people commit suicide every year in Japan. "The Suicide Prevention Website-Words of Truth for You-" presents spiritual prescriptions for worries such as depression, lost love, extramarital affairs, bullying and work-related problems, thereby saving many lives.

◆ **Support for Anti-bullying Campaigns**

Happy Science provides support for a group of parents and guardians, Network to Protect Children from Bullying, a general incorporated foundation launched in Japan to end bullying, including those that can even be called a criminal offense. So far, the network received more than 5,000 cases and resolved 90% of them.

- ◆ **The Golden Age Scholarship**

  This scholarship is granted to students who can contribute greatly and bring a hopeful future to the world.

- ◆ **Success No.1**
  Buddha's Truth Afterschool Academy

  Happy Science has over 180 classrooms throughout Japan and in several cities around the world that focus on afterschool education for children. The education focuses on faith and morals in addition to supporting children's school studies.

- ◆ **Angel Plan V**

  For children under the age of kindergarten, Happy Science holds classes for nurturing healthy, positive, and creative boys and girls.

- ◆ **Future Stars Training Department**

  The Future Stars Training Department was founded within the Happy Science Media Division with the goal of nurturing talented individuals to become successful in the performing arts and entertainment industry.

- ◆ **New Star Production Co., Ltd.**
  ARI Production Co., Ltd.

  We have companies to nurture actors and actresses, artists, and vocalists. They are also involved in film production.

ABOUT HAPPY SCIENCE MOVIES

BEAUTIFUL LURE
- A MODERN TALE OF "PAINTED SKIN"

Coming Soon

STORY With both beauty and wit, Maiko looks for a man who suits her. One night, she finds Taro, a candidate for the prime minister. Everything goes well as she plans, but Taro finds out that she is actually a "Youma", a foxy demon who destroys the country. What does fate hold for them?

64 Awards from 11 Countries!

USA
SPECIAL JURY REMI AWARD DRAMA
54th WorldFest Houston International Film Festival 2021

USA
GOLD REMI AWARD BEST ACTRESS ~ PANORAMA ASIA
54th WorldFest Houston International Film Festival 2021

USA
RUSSIAN-AMERICAN BUSINESS - BEST FOREIGN FEATURE FILM
54th WorldFest Houston International Film Festival 2021

UK
JURY AWARD
London International Cinema Festival 2021

*For more information, visit **www.beautifullure.com***

TWICEBORN
On VOD NOW

STORY Satoru Ichijo receives a message from the spiritual world and realizes his mission is to lead humankind to happiness. He becomes a successful businessman while publishing spiritual messages secretly, but the devil's temptation shakes his mind and...

ITALY
BEST DIRECTOR OF A FOREIGN LANGUAGE FEATURE FILM
[World Cinema Milan 2021]

SPAIN
BEST FOREIGN LANGUAGE FEATURE FILM
[Madrid International Film Festival 2020]

USA
BEST INTERNATIONAL FEATURE NOMINATION
[San Diego International Film Festival 2020]

UK
OFF-COMPETITION SPECIAL SCREENING
[Raindance Film Festival 2020]

41 Awards from 8 Countries!

*For more information, visit **www.twicebornmovie.com***

IMMORTAL HERO `On VOD NOW`

Based on the true story of a man whose near-death experience inspires him
to choose life... and change the lives of millions.

42 Awards from 9 Countries!

SPAIN
BARCELONA INTERNATIONAL
FILM FESTIVAL 2019
[THE CASTELL AWARDS]

SPAIN
MADRID INTERNATIONAL
FILM FESTIVAL 2019
[BEST DIRECTOR OF A FOREIGN
LANGUAGE FEATURE FILM]

ITALY
FLORENCE FILM AWARDS JUL 2019
[HONORABLE MENTION:
FEATURE FILM]

USA
INDIE VISIONS FILM FESTIVAL
JUL 2019 [WINNER (NARRATIVE
FEATURE FILM)]

ITALY
FLORENCE FILM AWARDS JUL 2019
[BEST ORIGINAL SCREENPLAY]

ITALY
DIAMOND FILM AWARDS JUL 2019
[WINNER (NARRATIVE
FEATURE FILM)]

...and more!

For more information, visit www.immortal-hero.com

THE REAL EXORCIST `On VOD NOW`

58 Awards from 9 Countries!

`STORY` Tokyo —the most mystical city in the world where
you find spiritual spots in the most unexpected places. Sayuri
works as a part-time waitress at a small coffee shop "Extra"
where regular customers enjoy the authentic coffee that the
owner brews. Meanwhile, Sayuri uses her supernatural powers
to help those who are troubled by spiritual phenomena one
after another. Through her special consultations, she touches
the hearts of the people and helps them by showing the truths
of the invisible world.

USA
GOLD REMI AWARD
53rd WorldFest Houston
International Film Festival 2020

MONACO
BEST FEATURE FILM
17th Angel Film Awards
2020
Monaco International Film Festival

NIGERIA
BEST FEATURE FILM
EKO International Film Festival
2020

THAI
BEST PRODUCTION DESIGN
Thai International Film Festival
2020

For more information, visit www.realexorcistmovie.com

ABOUT HAPPINESS REALIZATION PARTY

The Happiness Realization Party (HRP) was founded in May 2009 by Master Ryuho Okawa as part of the Happy Science Group to offer concrete and proactive solutions to the current issues such as military threats from North Korea and China and the long-term economic recession. HRP aims to implement drastic reforms of the Japanese government, thereby bringing peace and prosperity to Japan. To accomplish this, HRP proposes two key policies:

1) Strengthening the national security and the Japan-U.S. alliance, which plays a vital role in the stability of Asia.

2) Improving the Japanese economy by implementing drastic tax cuts, taking monetary easing measures and creating new major industries.

HRP advocates that Japan should offer a model of a religious nation that allows diverse values and beliefs to coexist, and that contributes to global peace.

*For more information, visit **en.hr-party.jp***

HAPPY SCIENCE ACADEMY
JUNIOR AND SENIOR HIGH SCHOOL

Happy Science Academy Junior and Senior High School is a boarding school founded with the goal of educating the future leaders of the world who can have a big vision, persevere, and take on new challenges.

Currently, there are two campuses in Japan; the Nasu Main Campus in Tochigi Prefecture, founded in 2010, and the Kansai Campus in Shiga Prefecture, founded in 2013.

Nasu Main Campus

Kansai Campus

HAPPY SCIENCE UNIVERSITY

THE FOUNDING SPIRIT AND THE GOAL OF EDUCATION

Based on the founding philosophy of the university, "Exploration of happiness and the creation of a new civilization," education, research and studies will be provided to help students acquire deep understanding grounded in religious belief and advanced expertise with the objectives of producing "great talents of virtue" who can contribute in a broad-ranging way to serve Japan and the international society.

FACULTIES

Faculty of human happiness

Students in this faculty will pursue liberal arts from various perspectives with a multidisciplinary approach, explore and envision an ideal state of human beings and society.

Faculty of successful management

This faculty aims to realize successful management that helps organizations to create value and wealth for society and to contribute to the happiness and the development of management and employees as well as society as a whole.

Faculty of future creation

Students in this faculty study subjects such as political science, journalism, performing arts and artistic expression, and explore and present new political and cultural models based on truth, goodness and beauty.

Faculty of future industry

This faculty aims to nurture engineers who can resolve various issues facing modern civilization from a technological standpoint and contribute to the creation of new industries of the future.

CONTACT INFORMATION

Happy Science is a worldwide organization with faith centers around the globe. For a comprehensive list of centers, visit the worldwide directory at *happy-science.org*. The following are some of the many Happy Science locations:

UNITED STATES AND CANADA

New York
79 Franklin St., New York, NY 10013
Phone: 212-343-7972
Fax: 212-343-7973
Email: ny@happy-science.org
Website: happyscience-usa.org

New Jersey
725 River Rd, #102B, Edgewater, NJ 07020
Phone: 201-313-0127
Fax: 201-313-0120
Email: nj@happy-science.org
Website: happyscience-usa.org

Florida
5208 8th St., Zephyrhills, FL 33542
Phone: 813-715-0000
Fax: 813-715-0010
Email: florida@happy-science.org
Website: happyscience-usa.org

Atlanta
1874 Piedmont Ave., NE Suite 360-C
Atlanta, GA 30324
Phone: 404-892-7770
Email: atlanta@happy-science.org
Website: happyscience-usa.org

San Francisco
525 Clinton St.
Redwood City, CA 94062
Phone & Fax: 650-363-2777
Email: sf@happy-science.org
Website: happyscience-usa.org

Los Angeles
1590 E. Del Mar Blvd., Pasadena, CA 91106
Phone: 626-395-7775
Fax: 626-395-7776
Email: la@happy-science.org
Website: happyscience-usa.org

Orange County
10231 Slater Ave., #204
Fountain Valley, CA 92708
Phone: 714-745-1140
Email: oc@happy-science.org
Website: happyscience-usa.org

San Diego
7841 Balboa Ave., Suite #202
San Diego, CA 92111
Phone: 626-395-7775
Fax: 626-395-7776
E-mail: sandiego@happy-science.org
Website: happyscience-usa.org

Hawaii
Phone: 808-591-9772
Fax: 808-591-9776
Email: hi@happy-science.org
Website: happyscience-usa.org

Kauai
3343 Kanakolu Street, Suite 5
Lihue, HI 96766, U.S.A.
Phone: 808-822-7007
Fax: 808-822-6007
Email: kauai-hi@happy-science.org
Website: happyscience-usa.org

Toronto

845 The Queensway
Etobicoke ON M8Z 1N6 Canada
Phone: 1-416-901-3747
Email: toronto@happy-science.org
Website: happy-science.ca

Vancouver

#201-2607 East 49th Avenue
Vancouver, BC, V5S 1J9, Canada
Phone: 1-604-437-7735
Fax: 1-604-437-7764
Email: vancouver@happy-science.org
Website: happy-science.ca

INTERNATIONAL

Tokyo

1-6-7 Togoshi, Shinagawa
Tokyo, 142-0041 Japan
Phone: 81-3-6384-5770
Fax: 81-3-6384-5776
Email: tokyo@happy-science.org
Website: happy-science.org

Seoul

74, Sadang-ro 27-gil,
Dongjak-gu, Seoul, Korea
Phone: 82-2-3478-8777
Fax: 82-2-3478-9777
Email: korea@happy-science.org
Website: happyscience-korea.org

London

3 Margaret St.
London,W1W 8RE United Kingdom
Phone: 44-20-7323-9255
Fax: 44-20-7323-9344
Email: eu@happy-science.org
Website: happyscience-uk.org

Taipei

No. 89, Lane 155, Dunhua N. Road
Songshan District, Taipei City 105, Taiwan
Phone: 886-2-2719-9377
Fax: 886-2-2719-5570
Email: taiwan@happy-science.org
Website: happyscience-tw.org

Sydney

516 Pacific Hwy, Lane Cove North,
NSW 2066, Australia
Phone: 61-2-9411-2877
Fax: 61-2-9411-2822
Email: sydney@happy-science.org

Malaysia

No 22A, Block 2, Jalil Link Jalan Jalil Jaya 2,
Bukit Jalil 57000, Kuala Lumpur, Malaysia
Phone: 60-3-8998-7877
Fax: 60-3-8998-7977
Email: malaysia@happy-science.org
Website: happyscience.org.my

Brazil Headquarters

Rua. Domingos de Morais 1154,
Vila Mariana, Sao Paulo SP
CEP 04009-002, Brazil
Phone: 55-11-5088-3800
Fax: 55-11-5088-3806
Email: sp@happy-science.org
Website: happyscience.com.br

Nepal

Kathmandu Metropolitan City Ward
No. 15,
Ring Road, Kimdol,
Sitapaila Kathmandu, Nepal
Phone: 97-714-272931
Email: nepal@happy-science.org

Jundiai

Rua Congo, 447, Jd. Bonfiglioli
Jundiai-CEP, 13207-340
Phone: 55-11-4587-5952
Email: jundiai@happy-science.org

Uganda

Plot 877 Rubaga Road, Kampala
P.O. Box 34130, Kampala, Uganda
Phone: 256-79-4682-121
Email: uganda@happy-science.org
Website: happyscience-uganda.org

ABOUT IRH PRESS

IRH Press Co., Ltd., based in Tokyo, was founded in 1987 as a publishing division of Happy Science. IRH Press publishes religious and spiritual books, journals, magazines and also operates broadcast and film production enterprises. For more information, visit *okawabooks.com*.

Follow us on:

Facebook: Okawa Books   **Twitter:** Okawa Books

Goodreads: Ryuho Okawa   **Instagram:** OkawaBooks

Pinterest: Okawa Books

——— NEWSLETTER ———

To receive book related news, promotions and events, please subscribe to our newsletter below.

https://okawabooks.us11.list-manage.com/subscribe?u=1fc70960eefd92668052ab7f8&id=2fbd8150ef

——— MEDIA ———

OKAWA BOOK CLUB

A conversation about Ryuho Okawa's titles, topics ranging from self-help, current affairs, spirituality and religions.

Available at iTunes, Spotify and Amazon Music.

Apple iTunes:
https://podcasts.apple.com/us/podcast/okawa-book-club/id1527893043

Spotify:
https://open.spotify.com/show/09mpgX2iJ6stVm4eBRdo2b

Amazon Music:
https://music.amazon.com/podcasts/7b759f24-ff72-4523-bfee-24f48294998f/Okawa-Book-Club

BOOKS BY RYUHO OKAWA

RYUHO OKAWA'S LAWS SERIES

The Laws Series is an annual volume of books that are mainly comprised of Ryuho Okawa's lectures on various topics that highlight principles and guidelines for the activities of Happy Science every year. *The Laws of the Sun*, the first publication of the laws series, ranked in the annual best-selling list in Japan in 1987. Since then, all of the laws series' titles have ranked in the annual best-selling list for more than two decades, setting socio-cultural trends in Japan and around the world.

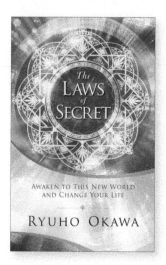

The 27th Laws Series

THE LAWS OF SECRET

AWAKEN TO THIS NEW WORLD AND CHANGE YOUR LIFE

Paperback • 248 pages • $16.95
ISBN: 978-1-942125-81-5

Our physical world coexists with the multi-dimensional spirit world and we are constantly interacting with some kind of spiritual energy, whether positive or negative, without consciously realizing it. This book reveals how our lives are affected by invisible influences, including the spiritual reasons behind influenza, the novel coronavirus infection, and other illnesses.

The new view of the world in this book will inspire you to change your life in a better direction, and to become someone who can give hope and courage to others in this age of confusion.

---

*For a complete list of books, visit **okawabooks.com***

THE TRILOGY

The first three volumes of the Laws Series, *The Laws of the Sun*, *The Golden Laws*, and *The Nine Dimensions* make a trilogy that completes the basic framework of the teachings of God's Truths. *The Laws of the Sun* discusses the structure of God's Laws, *The Golden Laws* expounds on the doctrine of time, and *The Nine Dimensions* reveals the nature of space.

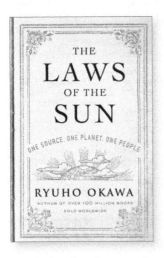

THE LAWS OF THE SUN

ONE SOURCE, ONE PLANET, ONE PEOPLE

Paperback • 288 pages • $15.95
ISBN: 978-1-942125-43-3

IMAGINE IF YOU COULD ASK GOD why He created this world and what spiritual laws He used to shape us—and everything around us. If we could understand His designs and intentions, we could discover what our goals in life should be and whether our actions move us closer to those goals or farther away.

At a young age, a spiritual calling prompted Ryuho Okawa to outline what he innately understood to be universal truths for all humankind. In *The Laws of the Sun*, Okawa outlines these laws of the universe and provides a road map for living one's life with greater purpose and meaning.

In this powerful book, Ryuho Okawa reveals the transcendent nature of consciousness and the secrets of our multidimensional universe and our place in it. By understanding the different stages of love and following the Buddhist Eightfold Path, he believes we can speed up our eternal process of development. *The Laws of the Sun* shows the way to realize true happiness—a happiness that continues from this world through the other.

---

*For a complete list of books, visit **okawabooks.com***

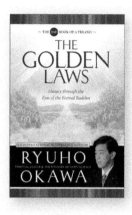

THE GOLDEN LAWS
HISTORY THROUGH THE EYES OF THE ETERNAL BUDDHA

Paperback • 201 pages • $14.95
ISBN: 978-1-941779-81-1

Throughout history, Great Guiding Spirits of Light have been present on Earth in both the East and the West at crucial points in human history to further our spiritual development. *The Golden Laws* reveals how Divine Plan has been unfolding on Earth, and outlines 5,000 years of the secret history of humankind. Once we understand the true course of history, through past, present and into the future, we cannot help but become aware of the significance of our spiritual mission in the present age.

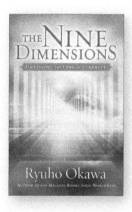

THE NINE DIMENSIONS
UNVEILING THE LAWS OF ETERNITY

Paperback • 168 pages • $15.95
ISBN: 978-0-982698-56-3

This book is a window into the mind of our loving God, who designed this world and the vast, wondrous world of our afterlife as a school with many levels through which our souls learn and grow. When the religions and cultures of the world discover the truth of their common spiritual origin, they will be inspired to accept their differences, come together under faith in God, and build an era of harmony and peaceful progress on Earth.

For a complete list of books, visit ***okawabooks.com***

THE LAWS OF HAPPINESS
LOVE, WISDOM, SELF-REFLECTION AND PROGRESS

Paperback • 264 pages • $16.95
ISBN: 978-1-942125-70-9

This book endeavors to answer the question, "What is true happiness?" This milestone text introduces four distinct principles, based on the "Laws of Mind" and sourced from Okawa's real-world experience, to guide readers towards sustainable happiness. Okawa's four "Principles of Happiness" present an easy, yet profound framework to ground this rapidly advanced and highly competitive society. In practice, Okawa outlines pragmatic steps to revitalize our ambition to lead a happier and meaningful life.

THE LAWS OF SUCCESS
A SPIRITUAL GUIDE TO TURNING YOUR HOPES INTO REALITY

Paperback • 208 pages • $15.95
ISBN: 978-1-942125-15-0

The Laws of Success offers 8 spiritual principles that, when put to practice in our day-to-day life, will help us attain lasting success and let us experience the fulfillment of living our purpose and the joy of sharing our happiness with many others. The timeless wisdom and practical steps that Ryuho Okawa offers will guide us through any difficulties and problems we may face in life, and serve as guiding principles for living a positive, constructive, and meaningful life.

---

*For a complete list of books, visit **okawabooks.com***

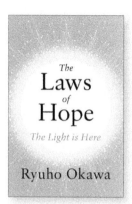

THE LAWS OF HOPE
THE LIGHT IS HERE

Paperback • 224 pages • $16.95
ISBN:978-1-942125-76-1

This book provides ways to bring light and hope to ourselves through our own efforts, even in the midst of sufferings and adversities. Inspired by a wish to bring happiness, success, and hope to humanity, Okawa shows us how to look at and think about our lives and circumstances. He says that hopes come true when we have the right mindset inside us.

THE LAWS OF JUSTICE
HOW WE CAN SOLVE WORLD CONFLICTS AND BRING PEACE

Paperback • 208 pages • $15.95
ISBN: 978-1-942125-05-1

This book shows what global justice is from a comprehensive perspective of the Supreme God. Becoming aware of this view will let us embrace differences in beliefs, recognize other people's divine nature, and love and forgive one another. It will also become the key to solving the issues we face, whether they're religious, political, societal, economic, or academic, and help the world become a better and safer world for all of us living today.

---

*For a complete list of books, visit **okawabooks.com***

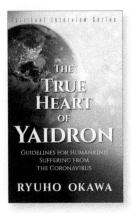

THE TRUE HEART OF YAIDRON
GUIDELINES FOR HUMANKIND SUFFERING FROM THE CORONAVIRUS

Paperback • 144 pages • $11.95
ISBN: 978-1-943928-04-0

What are the real cause and evil schemes behind the worldwide coronavirus crisis whose death tolls are now past 2.8 million? Out of compassion, this book reveals truths about the all-out global war now being waged by the evil power in East Asia that's destroying the power of the people. Discover the movement that's trying to bring together the powers of the West, India, and Asia by the belief of "With Savior," to save humankind and create the new golden future of Earth.

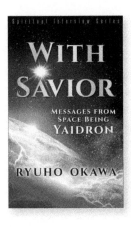

WITH SAVIOR
MESSAGES FROM SPACE BEING YAIDRON

Paperback • 232 pages • $13.95
ISBN: 978-1-943869-94-7

The human race is now faced with multiple unprecedented crises. Perhaps God is warning us humans to reconsider our materialistic and arrogant ways. Fortunately, God has sent us a savior, who is now teaching us to repent and showing us the path we should choose. In this book, space being Yaidron sends his warnings and messages of hope.

---

*For a complete list of books, visit **okawabooks.com***

LOVE FOR THE FUTURE
BUILDING ONE WORLD OF FREEDOM AND DEMOCRACY UNDER GOD'S TRUTH

Paperback • 312 pages • $15.95
ISBN: 978-1-942125-60-0

This is a compilation of select international lectures given by Ryuho Okawa during his (ongoing) global missionary tours. While conflicting values of justice exist, this book espouses freedom and democracy are vital principles for global unification that will resolutely foster peace and shared prosperity, if adopted universally.

CHINA'S HIDDEN AGENDA
THE MASTERMIND BEHIND THE ANTI-AMERICAN AND ANTI-JAPANESE PROTESTS

Paperback • 182 pages • $14.95
ISBN:978-1-937673-18-5

"I wanted to stir up the anti-American movement in the Arab world to make sure that the United States won't be able to attack Syria or Iran...I'm the mastermind behind the Muhammad video."

—Xi Jinping's Guardian Spirit

---

*For a complete list of books, visit **okawabooks.com***

HOW TO SURVIVE THE CORONAVIRUS RECESSION

Paperback • 171 pages • $14.95
ISBN: 978-1-943869-97-8

From the perspectives of both economics and health, this book delves into how you can survive the coronavirus recession. As taught by the author Ryuho Okawa, there is a strong relationship between your spiritual health and immunity, and he demonstrates the mindset you should have as well as introduces a very effective meditation that you can do to truly strengthen your immunity.

THE STRONG MIND

THE ART OF BUILDING THE INNER STRENGTH TO OVERCOME LIFE'S DIFFICULTIES

Paperback • 192 pages • $15.95
ISBN: 978-1-942125-36-5

The strong mind is what we need to rise time and again, and to move forward no matter what difficulties we face in life. This book will inspire and empower you to take courage, develop a mature and cultivated heart, and achieve resilience and hardiness so that you can break through the barriers of your limits and keep winning in the battle of your life.

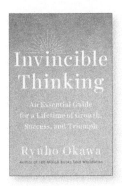

INVINCIBLE THINKING

AN ESSENTIAL GUIDE FOR A LIFETIME OF GROWTH, SUCCESS, AND TRIUMPH

Hardcover • 208 pages • $16.95
ISBN: 978-1-942125-25-9

In this book, Ryuho Okawa lays out the principles of invincible thinking that will allow us to achieve long-lasting triumph. This powerful and unique philosophy is not only about becoming successful or achieving our goal in life, but also about building the foundation of life that becomes the basis of our life-long, lasting success and happiness.

---

*For a complete list of books, visit **okawabooks.com***

HONG KONG REVOLUTION

SPIRITUAL MESSAGES OF THE GUARDIAN SPIRITS OF XI JINPING AND AGNES CHOW TING

Paperback • 282 pages • $13.95
ISBN: 978-1-943869-55-8

The Hong Kong protests that are gathering the attention of the world. What is Xi Jinping plotting? How far is Agnes Chow, the 'Goddess of Democracy,' willing to go? Their guardian spirits sreveal issues of conflict in this exciting new book!

SPIRITUAL INTERVIEW WITH THE GUARDIAN SPIRIT OF JOSHUA WONG

HIS RESOLVE TO PROTECT THE FREEDOM OF HONG KONG

Paperback • 82 pages • $9.95
ISBN:978-1-943869-54-1

To those around the world who believe in God and pray for God's justice to be served, we hereby bring you the words of the guardian spirit of Joshua Wong Let there be glory in his courage and the freedom of Hong Kong.

SPIRITUAL INTERVIEW WITH LIU XIAOBO

THE FIGHT FOR FREEDOM CONTINUES

Paperback • 128 pages • $9.95
ISBN:978-1-943869-25-1

On July 21, 2017, 8 days after his death, the spirit of Liu Xiaobo was resurrected to deliver his messages. This book reveals the truths about China, a totalitarian country that doesn't grant freedom to its people. In this book, the Chinese Nobel Prize winner shares his wish to hand down the movement of China's democratization to future generations.

*For a complete list of books, visit **okawabooks.com***

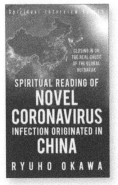

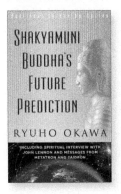

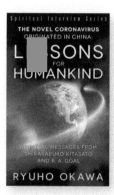

THE NOVEL CORONAVIRUS ORIGINATED IN CHINA: LESSONS FOR HUMANKIND

SPIRITUAL MESSAGES FROM SHIBASABURO KITASATO AND R. A. GOAL

Paperback • 228 pages • $13.95
ISBN: 978-1-943869-88-6

This book records spiritual messages from a bacteriologist and a space being. They disclose many truths about the novel coronavirus pandemic, such as China's hidden secrets, what the future holds, and hopeful messages for humanity. Only when humanity learns what we are to learn from this pandemic, can we escape this worldwide crisis and create a new age.

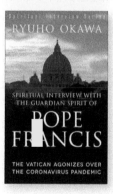

SPIRITUAL INTERVIEW WITH THE GUARDIAN SPIRIT OF POPE FRANCIS

THE VATICAN AGONIZES OVER THE CORONAVIRUS PANDEMIC

Paperback • 268 pages • $13.95
ISBN: 978-1-943869-84-8

In this book, the guardian spirit of Pope Francis confesses his hopelessness, goodwill, and limit as a human being amid the ongoing coronavirus pandemic. Are his prayers heard by Jesus? By also reading *Jesus Christ's Answers to the Coronavirus Pandemic*, you will be able to understand the true will of Jesus and the faith in true God.

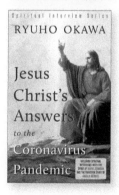

JESUS CHRIST'S ANSWERS TO THE CORONAVIRUS PANDEMIC

Paperback • 204 pages • $11.95
ISBN: 978-1-943869-81-7

In this book, the spirit of Jesus answers the causes, prospects, and coping strategies for the novel coronavirus pandemic. Instead of hoping for the development of an effective vaccine to come soon, we should use our spiritual power to defeat the evil thoughts that spiritually possess this virus. It's a book for all who believe in Jesus.

For a complete list of books, visit **okawabooks.com**

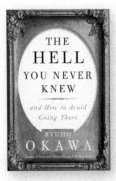

THE HELL YOU NEVER KNEW

AND HOW TO AVOID GOING THERE

Paperback • 192 pages • $15.95
ISBN: 978-1-942125-52-5

From ancient times, people have been warned of the danger of falling to Hell. But does the world of Hell truly exist? If it does, what kind of people would go there? Through his spiritual abilities, Ryuho Okawa found out that Hell is only a small part of the vast Spirit World, yet more than half of the people today go there after they die.

THE REAL EXORCIST

ATTAIN WISDOM TO CONQUER EVIL

Paperback • 208 pages • $16.95
ISBN:978-1-942125-67-9

This is a profound spiritual text backed by the author's nearly 40 years of real-life experience with spiritual phenomena. In it, Okawa teaches how we may discern and overcome our negative tendencies, by acquiring the right knowledge, mindset and lifestyle.

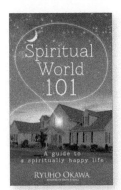

SPIRITUAL WORLD 101

A GUIDE TO A SPIRITUALLY HAPPY LIFE

Paperback • 184 pages • $14.95
ISBN: 978-1-941779-43-9

This book is a spiritual guidebook that will answer all your questions about the spiritual world, with illustrations and diagrams explaining about your guardian spirit and the secrets of God and Buddha. By reading this book, you will be able to understand the true meaning of life and find happiness in everyday life.

*For a complete list of books, visit **okawabooks.com***

THE TRUE EIGHTFOLD PATH
GUIDEPOSTS FOR SELF-INNOVATION

Paperback • 272 pages • $16.95
ISBN: 978-1-942125-80-8

This book explains how we can apply the Eightfold Path, one of the main pillars of Shakyamuni Buddha's teachings, as everyday guideposts in the modern-age to achieve self-innovation to live better and make positive changes in these uncertain times.

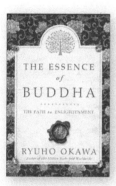

THE ESSENCE OF BUDDHA
THE PATH TO ENLIGHTENMENT

Paperback • 208 pages • $14.95
ISBN: 978-1-942125-06-8

In this book, Ryuho Okawa imparts in simple and accessible language his wisdom about the essence of Shakyamuni Buddha's philosophy of life and enlightenment–teachings that have been inspiring people all over the world for over 2,500 years. By offering a new perspective on core Buddhist thoughts, Okawa brings these teachings to life for modern people. This book distills a way of life that anyone can practice to achieve a life of self-growth, compassionate living, and true happiness.

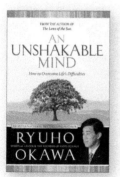

AN UNSHAKABLE MIND
HOW TO OVERCOME LIFE'S DIFFICULTIES

Paperback • 146 pages • $14.95
ISBN: 978-1-941779-67-5

This book describes ways to build inner confidence and achieve spiritual growth, adopting a spiritual perspective as the basis. With a willingness to learn from everything that life presents you, good or bad, any difficulty can be transformed into nourishment for the soul.

For a complete list of books, visit **_okawabooks.com_**

HEALING FROM WITHIN
Life-Changing Keys to Calm, Spiritual, and Healthy Living

THE LAWS OF HOPE
The Light is Here

THE STARTING POINT OF HAPPINESS
An Inspiring Guide to Positive Living with Faith, Love, and Courage

WORRY-FREE LIVING
Let Go of Stress and Live in Peace and Happiness

UFOS CAUGHT ON CAMERA!
A Spiritual Investigation on Videos and Photos
of the Luminous Objects Visiting Earth

THE MIRACLE OF MEDITATION
Opening Your Life to Peace, Joy, and the Power Within

THINK BIG!
Be Positive and Be Brave to Achieve Your Dreams

CHANGE YOUR LIFE, CHANGE THE WORLD
A Spiritual Guide to Living Now

INVITATION TO HAPPINESS
7 Inspirations from Your Inner Angel

---

*For a complete list of books, visit **okawabooks.com***

MUSIC BY RYUHO OKAWA

THE THUNDER

a composition for repelling the Coronavirus

We have been granted this music from our Lord. It will repel away the novel Coronavirus originated in China. Experience this magnificent powerful music.

Search on YouTube

the thunder coronavirus for a short ad!

THE EXORCISM

prayer music for repelling Lost Spirits

Feel the divine vibrations of this Japanese and Western exorcising symphony to banish all evil possessions you suffer from and to purify your space!

Search on YouTube

the exorcism repelling for a short ad!

WITH SAVIOR

English version

"Come what may, you shall expect your future"

This is the message of hope to the modern people who are living in the midst of the Coronavirus pandemic, natural disasters, economic depression, and other various crises.

Search on YouTube | with savior | for a short ad!

THE WATER REVOLUTION

English and Chinese version

"Power to the People!"

For the truth and happiness of the 1.4 billion people in China who have no freedom. Love, justice, and sacred rage of God are on this melody that will give you courage to fight to bring peace.

Search on YouTube | the water revolution | for a short ad!